Did I Tell You?

Did I Tell You?

131 POEMS FOR CHILDREN IN NEED

Edited by Nicky Gould and Vicky Wilson

WordAid.org.uk

First published in 2010 for WordAid.org.uk
by Categorical Books
70 Margate Road, Herne Bay, Kent CT6 7BH

For further information about this and other WordAid projects, please visit
www.wordaid.org.uk

All profits from book sales go to Children in Need
To order more copies, please send a cheque for £12 per copy (including
postage & packing) to Categorical Books at the above address or visit
www.wordaid.org.uk

British cataloguing in publication
A CIP record for this book is available from the British Library

ISBN 978-1-904662-11-2

Copyright © 2010 the contributors

Production assistant Becky King

Printed in Great Britain by Lightning Source

Section openers
I , II, VII, VIII George Andrews
III Jo Rutt, Nancy Wilson, Catherine Wright
IV Vici Cast, Jo Rutt, Nancy Wilson, Catherine Wright
V Hannah Agboola, Felix Fraser and Sylvie Fraser
Dannielle, Jason, Joseph and Sanam from Guston Primary School in Dover
Aimee, Archie, Harry, Harry, Hayden, Phoebe and Poppy from Sandown
Primary School in Deal
VI Amber from Sandown Primary School in Deal
IX Georgia Wright

Cover drawings
Jess Averbeck, Chloe Butcher, Vici Cast, Alicia Clifford, Catriona Dalton,
Callum Davis, Phillippa Dennison, Georgia Forsyth, Susan Hills, Siobhan
Lamb, Alice Newman, Mike Oakes, Oliver Rose, Jo Rutt, Bexy Williams,
Nancy Wilson and Catherine Wright
Anamol, Apsara, Cameron, Hemisa, Joshua, Lina, Luke, Mishal, Prawesh,
Simon and Yakima from Guston Primary School in Dover
Brandon, Courtney, Georgia, Hayden, Lily, Luke, Maisie, Megan, Olivia,
Peter, Ruby, Sam, Sam B., Teona, Tobias and Zoe from Sandown Primary
School in Deal

FOREWORD

When we first had the idea of putting together an anthology of poetry in aid of Children in Need we expected to produce something on a small scale with contributions drawn mainly from our local area of Kent. Then, like a child, the project grew and grew; and like proud parents we found ourselves standing on the sidelines, amazed at what we had set in motion, thrilled but somewhat bemused. We have been both moved and gratified as the poems have poured in from all over the world – from Europe, the US and Australia as well as from distant parts of the UK. We would like to thank all those who sent us their work, as well as those who passed on our call for contributions to friends and colleagues.

In the end we received almost 400 poems and spent many hours debating which ones to publish. Our final selection ranges from work donated by famous poets to poems from new writers. Apart from the quality of the poetry, one of the delights for us has been that the writing provides such a vivid insight into childhood from so many different perspectives, with poems that evoke the joy and misery, physical poverty and emotional richness, fun and frustration, powerlessness and resilience that make up children's and adolescents' lives.

In addition to the poets, we would like to thank the many children who contributed artwork for the cover and section openings, and the teachers who supported them in doing so. Also our friends, families and the other members of WordAid who have given their time to the project.

Did I Tell You?... Please continue to spread the word to enable us to sell books and raise money.

Nicky Gould
Vicky Wilson

CONTENTS

The day stretches ahead – nothing but
grass and sky grass and sky grass and sky grass and sky
as far as the eye can see

nothing
but
sky and grass sky and grass sky and grass sky and grass

and the wind galloping hard over the fields
like a riderless horse.

Esther Morgan

DUSKY

I sat by the rhubarb patch, knowing sooner or later,
I'd be asked to nurse a brother injured in action
by invisible bullets. I'd already scribbled red-crosses
onto crepe paper, transformed my clothes into uniform.

I carried a plastic stethoscope in my lunch box,
carved medication notes onto tree trunks,
pressurised wounded arms, removed bandannas
from sweaty heads, replaced them with daisy-chained crowns.

The light reigned over us; the last trip of freedom
against wooden gunshot, our feet falling
into the rabbit holes we could no longer see to avoid.
Those frenzied moments between dusk and being forced inside.

Dorothy Fryd

Give me the room with the tangerine door, where the glossed-over gloop hung
from its hinge in a bubble-like drop never to rain, fighting prods – creased, but
not bursting. Back to the bum-wide sill, platooned with snipers in moulded
poses – down-on-one-kneers bombed by Airfix dangling in full Humbrol glory,
diving in lamp-post, gap-curtained, searchlight. Show me the Black Magic
secrets – the boxed world of garden live under the bed, where beetles mugged
snails as they leaked ever traywards, and ants made unsquashable, shagpile
escapes. Take me to where homemade shelving ascended the woodchip like
Sherpa Tenzing, as Commandos and Williams built temples of worship, and
everything important was brought into play – and all that mattered was right
here, today.

Gary Studley

IMPROMPTU

Now the kids are summer wolves, they rove
and bark, green growls ornate in the belting sun.

Their wet noses part the webbed grass, paws pad
towards the cool of a forest where they forage

in leaf-rugs, shout at cricket and woodlouse,
sing howls to the heights of creaking rafters.

Wood's bones clack rhythm to the jangle
of hooting boys, squirrels scutter wide-eyed

at the hammering chorus. And it rains.
Notes shake from canopy, glissando down

onto bobbing heads that bounce home, footprints
the quavers of an impromptu score.

Duncan Hall

The biting wind, the freezing sea
in August
in Polperro, Pendoggett, Port Isaac, Penzance;
my father and I ready for action
in modest bathing trunks
and scratchy swimsuit,
braving the elements, come what may;
my mother in a deckchair huddled
and wrapped in half-a-dozen jackets,
the car rug round her knees,
a red beret and sunglasses
and always the crossword.

One summer at Polzeath we tasted
chocolate mint ice-cream
for the very first time,
the three of us promenading across
deserted sands, munching our booty;
that year we stayed in a caravan
called 'Lucky Dip'
and the wind almost blew us off the clifftop
on the second night,
and my mother put her back out
shaking the doormat.

Other places, other discoveries;
multi-coloured sand on the Isle of Wight,
fossils in a bay near Lyme Regis,
and, at last,
finding a friend at the farmhouse in Chard,
walking our make-believe dogs across endless fields
talking about their characteristics,
turning into dogs ourselves
barking all the way back to the farm.

Clare Dawes

When the other kids tell you to get lost,
go build a sand train in the middle of the park.

Take spades, trowels, chisels, rasps;
buckets and pots for carrying water.

Coarse sand works best for chassis and boiler;
finer grains for the pistons, rods, axles.

Find a hollowed-out tree trunk for the funnel,
a large smooth marble to use as the dome.

Fashion the couplings from filigreed
willow leaves and oak branches.

Raid the bottle bank for windows and dials.
Ignore raised eyebrows when you rip up benches.

Reforge the slide, swings and roundabout as rails.
Recycle fence planks and gravel as sleepers and ballast.

Let the finishing touch be the coke-can whistle
that sings your departure. And not a moment

too soon, as the tender is crumbling
and the park-keeper's arrived, scratching his head.

Brian Edwards

my mum said
don't go down the rec
stay in the yard
I'll check
if you're there
and if you're not
by heck
you'll get it in the neck
when your dad gets back

my mum said
don't go down the park
now it's
getting dark
just you mark
my words
dad's bite is worse
than his bark

my Dad and me
we picked up the ball
sneaked out the back
and away
to the rec
'What the heck!'

said my Dad
with a flick
and a kick
it was wicked
in the park playing
footie in the dark

Jenny Kendrick

Somebody drove you.
No.
Yes, they did. She couldn't
walk so far. Why won't you
tell us?
But she did.
We did.
Together.
First we walked cautiously,
trying to look as though
we didn't exist.
But then we ran – shouting,
laughing, free.
Free.
Everywhere we looked
was somewhere new.
Somewhere we had never seen
and where no one had seen
us.
No classroom, no desks.
No one to tell us we were wrong.
We never felt hunger,
or thirst.
And her short leg worked just as well
as her other one.
We walked and walked,
walking away our lives.
Of course they brought us back.
Red brick and punishment.
Never to talk to each other again.
Of course we still do.
And life is just the same.
Only it isn't.
Because that day we achieved
the impossible.
We became more than they said
we could
be.
We.
Ran.

Helen Davis

One of the worst
of the random rules of grown-ups
was that thing
done to children on summer evenings,

when they would
make you go on up to bed, tapping
their watches,
starting to get really, really cross.

Lying there,
you watched the late sun rip through curtains,
striping the walls;
listened to birds singing their heads off.

Voices below
in the garden, clinking and laughter.
Big boys larking
out on the street, yelling their daft games.

You seethed there,
wishing away the long prison years
until you, too,
could stay out all night under the stars.

Jenny Mayor

Scissor-snips;
the music stand rejigs
its metal and accepts the role of handmaiden.
After bedtime on a summer's evening, I lie
eyes wide and gather clues
like poppies.

The stool stiffens
prim under the piano.
Pages of Massenet cut to the chase.
The violin case snaps: a conductor's baton, tapping,
its swell-bellied treasure
craving a tune.

No one will sing
though throats clear, pedals pump, fifths redress.
A shoe taps tempo; Dad's voice clocks *two, three, four.*
Hush. My sister's arpeggios roll in the dusk.
On this floor curtains swell, pillows fill,
I count too.

No need for sheep.
Meditation from Thaïs
clouds me in sleep. Lids drop like fingers
on keys, bow on strings. Slink out to play,
daytime is laughing out there,
spirited.

Mary Scheurer

It must have been old mother Deakin
who snitched on us, eyes swivelling
in a face like a bowl of dripping, bulk spread
over her doorstep, needles working
while something grey knits itself.

We bunk little brother over a wall
not tempted this week by Sunshine Corner,
picture-stamps of Jesus, a story –
the feeding of thousands like last year's outing
of fish-paste sandwiches, Dymchurch, the rain.

Snaking through alleyways to the shop
we press our faces against the glass
like jelly-babies in a jar, rush to the river,
listen for the hour – four chimes from St George's,
turn back, slap, into its hoarding:

Conscience is The Voice of God...

His booming drums at my stomach –
I've spent His tuppence. Sticky fingers
grime my lilac dress, the Blanco
on canvas shoes betrays grass stains.
I've played on the waste ground.

Gillian Moyes

I
wield
a long
handled spoon
too big for my hands
stand by the yellow Formica
topped table ready to meet it
eye to eye
this
swirling mountain
of soft whipped cream
sprinkled with cheap
crunchy nuts
drizzled with sticky red syrup
squash each sweet mouthful
juices round my lips
licked and spread
to spill down my chin
onto my shirt
dig deep with my
long handled spoon to
reach into the melting
ice cream mess
with soggy cubes of
canned fruit
and cherries.
I so need
to reach
the
very
last
lick
I am eight

the joy of my first
knicker bocker glory

Margaret Swan

I imagine you
in your bedroom:
door shut,
mum downstairs,

empty case
on your
Spiderman
duvet cover;

clear, glossy,
thick enough
to harbour
a goldfish;

the video itself
in the video player.

I bet you thought
Robin Hood
was a fox
in a green hat
with a waistcoat
or something

and felt reassured
by the pure
blocks of colour
that filled
the simple trapezoid
of the head of the Sheriff of Nottingham.

And I bet as you
slid through the
landscapes meeting
none of the sharp
edges that a
pencil stroke presents,

you did not feel
the hypocrisy
of the rich
or the union
of the slighted
common man

as I did in Moscow,
eating ice-cream
in my jim-jams,
with my granddad,

Robin Hood
on the brown
living-room TV.

Kyrill Potapov

DARK ANONYMITY

I was I in a huge sweeping dress
dancing with the king.
Burt Lancaster, on a high-flying swing,
caught me in his arms.
My hand felt the slap from Billy Bigelow.
I flew in planes with busters of dams,
without legs, I reached for the sky.

I was the bride a brother liked best,
I shot it out in a dusty town out west.
I cried on that frightening, sombre hill
keeping close the robe of red.
I dropped three coins in a fountain in Rome.
In my overlarge 1950s American home
I was Rock Hudson and Doris Day.

A child held spellbound
by the flickering shaft of light
in the darkness
I am still drawn into (on a bright afternoon).

Lesley Fuller

We only bought them in the first place as he is so bright;
we thought they'd give a stimulus his school can't quite supply -
No – I'm sorry – David doesn't want to play tonight -

We never for a moment dreamt he'd take to them in quite
this way – but then some boys are like that with anything they try.
We only bought them in the first place as he is so bright.

He's no trouble in the morning – up as soon as it is light;
evenings we hardly see him – when tea's done, off he'll fly –
No – I'm sorry – David doesn't want to play tonight -

The teacher who makes out he falls asleep in class, pays slight
attention to her, shows no will to learn – she should drop by!
We only bought them in the first place as he is so bright.

I admit we hoped a little modern culture, you know, might
unite him with the other boys – he's always been so shy –
No – I'm sorry – David doesn't want to play tonight –

But every time we ask him, he insists he's quite all right;
and our David is no fool. After all, we can't deny
we only bought them in the first place as he is so bright –
No – I'm sorry – David doesn't want to play tonight –

Caroline Price

I left him living with my Mum and Dad.
I liked to think of him squashed on my bed
beside the piano; chewing liquorice
allsorts; finding the white china ponies,
in my trunk, with his; listening to swifts
build their nests in the eaves.

The authorities then put a stop to it.
Elephants are always denied access
to homes in the countryside, they wrote.
But he's always lived there, I protested.
He's no danger to flora, fauna or strangers.
My pleas were rejected.

He moved out, seduced by a witch.
Mum whispered, *He's gone*: a crack in her voice.
It took time but I did track them down,

to a brand-new apartment in town: silent
and stinking of cabbage. He was shivering;
wrapped in her shawl, in the gloom of a room
at the top of a high-rise.
The curtains stayed closed up all day.
(She'd not have him see the lines on her face,
the grey in her hair or that wart on her chin!)
I had to sneak him away.

Squeezing him into the lift was a struggle.

I bought him a phone and a home overlooking
the sea! Now we speak every day
he says he's Okay.
Lonely?
Maybe.

When I visit, he unbolts the door
with the tip of his tusk. We stroll down to
the sun-drenched shore: past the jelly-bean huts
to the breakwater.

Curling up against the heat-wave,
he flaps his great ears to cool me,
and sprays water, like soda, all over
my head, feet and hands.

We sift memories together, like sand.

Alison McNaught

There are twenty-seven folds
in an origami crane.
You know each shape,
each line,
corners together,
thumbnail creasing,
following the lines,
turning your paper square
first one way, then the other,
forming diagonals,
diamonds, squares,
until the tiny replica appears.

Beside the water,
the great bird stands,
imperial, unmoving,
waiting, watching
as you keep folding
squares of paper,
folded paper prayers
for life.

You need one thousand
squares of paper
folded twenty-seven times
to make a thousand cranes,
with their fabled promise
of a granted wish.
You keep folding
squares of paper.
You hang them round your room
like votive offerings
but the sun sets early,
the days are short.

Beside the water
the great bird stirs
as you stop folding,
feathers tinged with autumn gold
on vast wings fanning,
lifting, gliding, flying free
as squares of coloured paper
tumble to the ground.

Margaret Beston

II

after the poem, 'A Boy's Head' by Miroslav Holub

In it there is a dream
that was started
before she was born,

and there is a globe
with hemispheres
which shall be happy.

There is her own spacecraft,
a chosen dress
and pictures of her friends.

There are shining rings
and a maze of mirrors.

There is a diary
for surprise occasions.

There is a horse springing hooves
across the sky.

There is a sea
that tides and swells
and cannot be mapped.

There is untold hope
in that no equation exactly
fits a head.

Katherine Gallagher

Armchairs lift their hind legs and totter
forward like human hand-walkers.
Curious as cows coming all round
the furniture fenced from the bones of the dead
branches, crashing in flakes to the ground.
Baddy slung his slipper overhead.
Ma-ma rescued it from the coal bed.

He's hardly been gone thru the yard
door. Where is one shoe, slightly charred?
Months pass and Ma-ma asks: *What stops the rains
running away?* She lifts a grid guard:
some furry thing rots in its burrow, the drain.
The beastie, that clad Baddy, won't nip toes again.

Richard Lung

THAT'S ME!

That's *me* in the book, Sir. On page twenty-two.
I'm looking for someone and maybe it's *you?*
I'm there every month, like a *'Wanted – Free Home'*.
And if nobody takes me, I'll grow up alone.

They use books like this to sell puppies and cats,
cage birds and reptiles and fancy white rats.
Books that sell horses and pigs, cows and sheep.
Pay the right price and they're yours, Sir, to keep.

There's no *'price'* for me. Well, not really in cash.
But an offer to take me must never be rash.
I was taken before and it didn't go well.
I wanted a home. But I only got hell.

Look, I'm not a kitten, a pup or a bird.
To expect me to beg would be really absurd.
No, don't turn the page, Sir. Please look at my face.
Can't you take me away from this horrible place?

Bob Le Vaillant

*Inspired by 'Children Who Wait', a magazine profiling children available for adoption
published by charity Adoption UK.*

Will one nasturtium do,
growing in the sad
window, valiantly putting out
its blooms, one by one,

its dead straw tendrils
with resistant roots pinched
between two fingers?
Child, ghost-child, here's a map:

a courtyard, a circular path
round which three wheels
tricycle forever.
In courtyard after courtyard

the child has sat, gravitating
to wysteria walls, geraniums
under single trees, like an animal
to her natural habitat.

It is the silence
that is her home – silence
of fallen leaves, the fallen leaves
that congregate in corners.

Mimi Khalvati

He is walking a line; his footsteps mark a square
around the playground. The others forget his name:
a boy that isn't really anywhere.

Wherever he was just then, he isn't there
but somewhere further along, just out of frame.
He is walking a line; his footsteps mark a square

enclosing his teacher, enclosing the autumn air.
She blames no one, knowing she cannot blame
a boy that isn't really anywhere.

He is more than alone. While other children pair
off by the fence and a penalty kicker takes aim,
he is walking a line. His footsteps mark a square

like the edge of a board, a game of solitaire.
He doesn't seem to know another game.
A boy that isn't really anywhere

is on the perimeter. You'd think he doesn't care
about being different. But still, and just the same,
he is walking a line; his footsteps mark a square,
a boy, that isn't really anywhere.

Ros Barber

Some children have that scapegrace look,
as though they fell through the cracks
and learned to live there;

preternaturally knowing,
quivering, vigilant,
readers of signs and portents;

alert to changes in pressure,
they dodge the blow before it falls,
usually; their lapses

in timing or concentration
are written on their bodies,
a manuscript continually corrected.

Some children, all the effort
goes into naming them.

David Callin

Here the windows of the portacabin
are open, no breeze passes through
as you dart from instrument to instrument,

exploring the tautness of the African drum,
playing with the dulcet sound of the triangle,
beating a pulse on the xylophone.

You peer through thick lenses that blur
your vision, you crash and stumble
in heavy trainers, sit cross-legged in torn leggings

oblivious of everything. Is there chaos in your head?
Frantically you rearrange cacti, spider plants,
humming guttural patterns, uneasy in the body

which you scarcely fit into. I'm turning
the rainstick, celebrating the rhythms of now,
but you're back with your grandmother,

the St Lucia sun baking you hot with sweat
and the smell of work you loved.
We start singing and there's me

trying to synchronise your energy
as we play out the morning sun.

                    *

Eating candyfloss we sit on the sea wall
near the hospital bus. The lamp-posts
were touching points from bus to beach.

Dazed eyes say medication's kicked in.
To our right, the pier with its amusements,
a steady noise protecting silence.

A child cries. His foot's cut and his mother
has her back to him. You talk about your brother,
his football team, and the pastor who takes him

to matches now your father's left. My brother's eight,
you say. Don't know about football so I choose words
and throw a pebble at the incoming tide but it doesn't reach.

Your mum and dad love you, I say.
Quit the crap, you say. Race you to the sea.

Wendy French

For the last performance the benches were full
and Liam was a Calling Bird, one of Four,
two boys and two girls, divided like Turtle Doves.

She pointed him out and at once
I saw the resemblance, the turn of the nose,
a mist in the blues of their eyes,
her pride in him almost maternal.

She didn't know what she'd get for Christmas
and agreed it would be a surprise,
didn't mention she couldn't be sure
which house she'd be in for the holiday

though she did say she'd loved this school
and how she'd brought him in
when she started Year Three, and later

their sister and little brother too, and did still,
dropped them off on the way, there was time
so it was OK and, yes, she liked to join in
with clubs and things like she did with the chorus

when the Master of the Rings fell head over heels
and Mr Partridge broke the spell and the dancers
gave it all they had to give and more, like her.

Michael Curtis

The in-between spaces
are where I belong

not to
this friend
that carer

this room
that shelter

this school
that town

this culture
that collective

this group of rebels
that group of conformists.

Between the walls
there is stillness,
and space to be.

Lorraine Spiro

To escape the thick, black night
of fearful dream-lit sleep,
I scurry quietly into the bathroom
and shut the door.

I kill the monstrous darkness
with an urgent tug of the cord
and staunch the tell-tale flow of light
with a towel and

stem the light bleeding through the
keyhole with another towel on the door
before I stop holding my breath for fear
of waking them.

If they find me they will scold me and
send me back to the blackness
of my bed. This is my halfway house
of cold comfort.

Here, I conquer one fear and hide
from another. I take up my seat on the
laundry box and wait for grey dawn to spill
under the blind.

Andrea Shieber

I was the prince here: a small boy
in short trousers with a half-crown haircut,
striped school tie and his shirt-tail hanging out,
socks and shoes in hand for knee-deep paddling.
The beach has hardly changed: the Isle on the skyline,
the same oncoming waves, the same pebbles underfoot,
some flat and good for skimming, some stained
with tar, others glistening or masked in sand,
drilled clean through by tidal awls or sucked concave,
bird's-egg-speckled or veined like ore, red
and pink and green, slate-black or gullback-grey.
And this is the great stone, round and weighty,
which my father lifted with a swipe of his instep,
like a 1950s centre scoring a goal from the circle,
to crash the shin of someone he'd thought leering at my mum,
the single time I saw my gentle dad disturb the peace.

Was it an ugly or a noble thing? I know the sun went in
and my parents didn't speak for the rest of the afternoon,
backs to the breakwater. With a million weapons all around,
the bones of my enemies half-buried in the mud,
                                        their destroyed craft
still thrashing in the waves and splintering,
                    I stood on the shore and stoned the sea.

Derek Sellen

When my father has almost gone he comes back again
as the child who accidentally bit off his own tongue

and brought it to his mother at the kitchen table
so she might fetch the doctor to sew it on again.

She stares at him and asks what he is holding.
He cannot say, or how this came to pass.

Andrew Motion

THE GARDEN

I slip unseen,
their wounding words
become muted as I leave.

A storm is coming, exquisite tremor
as thunder tumbles like rocks and
inky clouds seep nearer.

Trees rouse, stroke the sky, darts
of unmown grass, dip and dive.
The wind steals my breath
in a lover's kiss.

Rain spatters, casting damp stains,
adding and multiplying until
I can no longer hear
their angry voices.

Debbie Turner

Don't think it was all '*Shut it!*'
in our house,

go back to the time when the dog
was sick

and they nursed him all night
with sips of brandy,

to when snow filled the yard
and I was sent out

with mash and bran for Bobtail
the rabbit,

to the sprigs of chickweed she picked
for our budgie

and the seed and lard ball tied to the tree
with string.

Don't think when they died
no one cared,

the grief couldn't get past the gate
that's all.

Maggie Sawkins

A bedtime rhyme clings to me:
a long-lashed crab
an anemone with
glued-on glitter, and some
thing called a bristle worm
languid, ambiguously hairy
hybrid arms and heads in the bed
delicate tentacles self-sporing
and the pulsing crustacean's fontanel softness

Here come the worry dolls
little stick arms outstretched
and badly made clothes unravelling
like mummies advancing towards us
they carry a paper standard
an amulet in the adult alphabet
transcribed from a bedside interview
in a firm clear hand:
'I want my daddy to be my friend'
the poor stick man spells o what to do
sits on the pillow and swallows
the paper in pills

There is an equation to describe:
wanting daddy can only be solved
by adding daddy
which makes you want daddy
too long to be taught in school
with its problems that only school can solve
like why a protractor and compass sharp fear

the primate stands with the tin-opener hands
infected with mumps and mercury
tapping, helloing at our shell
our home for three

  Megan Watkins

in those always days of ships' holds
and table legs, an aniseed of dread
would wedge between milk teeth
evading bedtime brushing

a gob-stopping, puff-candy fear
which wore py-jams just like mine
between the sides-to-middled sheets

from the rug of Turkey red
I swum cold linoleum to check
the binary breathing of the double bed

in almost adolescence, of vinyl
and omnipotence, folk from when
Let's Twist Again was not around
seemed as good as drowned

Rachel Woolf

A fat-bellied
spavin-hocked
dirty white mare
droops among the scuttling chickens
near the five-barred gate.

A lilac bush,
climbable syringia
lace scenting the sky,
a crow's nest for a six year old
from which to view
a sea of shades of green.

To watch for the furtive fox,
the milkman, the coalman,
hide from the gipsies,
and hope, hope
to see the Onion Man.

The Onion Man!
popping sharply over the hill,
freewheeling down the pebble-peppered lane,
between the high-ferned hedges,
red hands clutching black bike handgrips,
wiry wheels spinning.

His strings of onions
laced over crouched shoulders
like strings of mermaid kelp.
Did his bike leap in one go from Brittany,
or did he swim across, the bike strapped to his back?

'He comes from Brittany on a boat,'
my parents say.

But surely that could not be true.
No boat could ferry such a hero.
A mere passenger? With a ticket and a suitcase?
My idea was best.

Parents don't know everything.

Val Doyle

When I wasn't the me that I am
but somebody else

and darted wild in the field
like a ferret in corn,

when I scattered the hours of my joy
as seeds to the wind,

chasing the cartwheeling sun
down the shouts of my days;

when I hid from the juggernaut years
in a jungle of stalks,

rocking cots woven into the reeds
of the scarlet-splashed wheat,

with the babes half an inch soft
and blind as my mind was then,

Dionysus drunk with the scents
of the blood-red dusk – when I

was just who I was in a field
and everything else over a stile, then

the shade of the Lurker rippled chill
through the feathered air

and stained the corn violet with pain
poured from a future phial

and the field was no longer a haven
but a minefield of holes in my brain,

leaking frights from a flood barely stemmed
by a jerry-built dyke, so I

abandoned the babes in the straw
and ducked down into the maze,

dodging the shades closing in
and the groping fingers of fate

and ran to the lights in my home,
shedding my breath in the dark

and slammed the door hard on what
would be one day for somebody else.

When that day I would be who I am
and not who I was.

Gabriel Griffin

The summer I conquer water, I taste power again
like learning to walk, but this time I'll remember –
being that proud impossible thing, a swimmer;
ecstatic, buoyed up, striking out and out,
swooping with the waves, diving through.

I flip to look back, and the beach is painting-
by-numbers – coloured patches so small I can't tell
which are my family. I was one of those bright dots
and now my space has closed behind me.
I could not exist, and there'd be no difference.

The sea starts to jostle and leer, I've swallowed
knowledge more serious than I knew there was.
This is too vast for me, and I'm swimming hard,
but the dots and patches don't get bigger. No point
shouting, I am invisible – too far out for anything

but keeping on, though without hope, with no
breath, and aching arms. But my life so far
doesn't pass before me like the teacher said, and now
my feet nudge seaweed, and I wade, jelly-legged
and look for our umbrella, and find it.

Nothing has happened. They haven't missed me.
It's cold. My knitted swimsuit is bleeding magenta
into powder blue. My parents set up cricket stumps.
They don't know it's all the same who wins.
The sun makes them cheerful. I am so much older.

Carole Satyamurti

A pink striped sailor's suit,
gingham dirndl, a dogtooth coat –
even once, a denim bikini.

So many outfits there've been
my progress mapped and measured
in cool, smooth tailor's chalk,

until the day I stood fidgeting
in paisley needlecord, all shades of red,
my mother pinning me at the hemline:
stay still, stay still why don't you...

Realising that although the dress was perfect,
I no longer fit.

Frances Knight

MY FATHER'S CLOTHES

Because I am taller now
and not quite pretty,
and because I like philosophy and grunge,
I borrow his clothes.
I visit his flat like a department store,
stock up on lowslung jeans and chunky knits
and flannel shirts, tobacco-scented.

Serious, androgynous,
I lope through college.
I roll up sleeves like I mean business,
my bumps and angles blurred through cord and wool,
his thick dark layers.
I've filled the house with him again,
and silently mum washes out the smell,
the shape of him in knees and elbows.

The flat is brown and temporary.
His drawers are stuffed with what I leave behind.
Patterned dresses, pairs of tights,
silk scarves and lacy socks. My old school pinafore.

Rachel Playforth

I live in childhood.
I build my wishes there like houses.
I add extensions. There are no foundations.
I hide in the basement and count thunderclaps.

I measure out the steps in the garden to find buried treasure,
I dig until I fall asleep. I have not found what I am looking for yet.
I go upstairs and try on clothes from the master bedroom,
I wave at myself reflected in baggy dresses and long gloves.
          And no shoes at all.
I never brush my hair. Do not really like to wash it.
I do not like to waste my pocket money on underwear. And stuff.

 I have parties in my room
          And all the pretend people I invite always come.
I play in the kitchen with oil and onion
          And cake.
          And when I am waiting for rice to boil, or mix to rise, I dance on
the lino.

I make up stories.
I am stubborn.
I do not want to be a good girl.
I do and do not want everyone to like me. Right now.
I am scared of my own thinking in the dark,
I do not like going to bed.
...I do not understand...
I want hugs. All the time. But only on my terms.
I want you to look at me. Are you watching?
Look at me.
Look. At me.

Emma Smith

Moving to senior school, aged eleven,
intrigued to find toilets with incinerators,
I asked my mum why they were needed.

She ferreted out a booklet and muttered
about changing, bleeding, big white knickers
with buckles to keep pads in place.

Miss Cornelius taught reproduction in Biology,
in Needlework, stitching, we pinned down
which girls had and which girls wouldn't.

I learnt much more when I discovered
Lady Chatterley's Lover in the bedroom cupboard,
read it, each night, under my covers.

Nancy Charley

One day, when my breasts were still thinking about it,
and I woke my older sister in the morning,
I asked her *but where do you put them at night?*
She told me – *Don't worry. They sort themselves out.*
I imagined them ducking her upper arms as she tossed and turned
and, when she rolled over, levering themselves out from under her sides.
Soon, I was carrying mine behind a shield, I thought, of folded arms,
turning their whispers into a shout.

What exciting lives they've led!
Hers have four children between them. Her twin
has four daughters and they have six children between them.
So many breasts and kisses! Such kisses.
All the love, and the years flown and I still don't know...
How they keep safe? Where they go?

Anne Stewart

HER ON THE CORNER

There's a chest she had. 'Breasts' they were called
They swelled up from her belt
aimed as straight as a pair of five inchers.

On her head was a beehive, yellow as scrambled egg
or the *Canary* square in my Rowney paintbox.

At night, me smoking sweet cigarettes in bed,
I would hear her walking out with the real thing
hanging from her lip. *To meet men*, Mrs Pym said,

Them stilettos could stab through working men's boots.
I'm sure she was right. Their sound ricocheted off the houses
like the guns were firing from under her blouse.

Vanessa Gebbie

Her words are modulated and
creep like the creek water
through mud and grass by the culvert
where tadpoles clutch stems with foetus legs.
Rose has fried an egg and left a plate
overturned on top 'to keep it warm, Honey,'
while she talks, her hand on a glass of Gallo,
nails as red as chipped porcelain petals
tapping the kitchen tiles to Peggy Lee.

The top half of her glass is tinted green
like old sunglasses, finger-printed and filled
with red that looks brown under the reflection
from the windows and a blot of lipstick.
The base of the glass, made of concentric circles
of clear glass marbles, reflects my face
again and again and again
as it rises, slowly tilting, circled by fingers
echoing the glass curve, urgently clutching.

Rose talks of the dead and nods carefully after each
sentence of death. She hums and smiles and her lips are
coated in two perfect bows of red that cracks,
while her eyes look aside as if the room were full of dancers.
She gives an anecdote about each in turn
and her voice hardens as the hours dance by.
In the long afternoon, tree-frogs sing in the garden
but they hide in the grass and are marked like the
leaves of the roses with black-spot.

In late summer the creek suddenly sparks with tiny frogs
springing like July fireworks as the dog runs through.
I catch them by the dozen, brown, green and metallic gold,
like treasure, some with tiny tails. If you rub their bellies
they fall asleep with legs in the air, throats pulsing.
When I saw Rose last, she lay in the parking lot
in front of the drugstore on her back,
arms and legs in the air, but still moving.
I was six, and a strange woman was screaming at me
'tell me her name little boy!'

Mark Holihan

I'm following my cousin and some chap:
they're checking, making sure no one's in sight.
My job's to figure out exactly why –
we're on the cliff path heading for the sea –
they're the target, I'm the *Silent-Spy* –
I saw it at the cinema last night.

9.20 – suspects whispering together,
they've crept off down a side path, looking sly
(they're what Gran calls, well matched, 'birds of a feather').
This spying's perilous, but 'do or die'.

Look out, they've gone to ground and so have I –
I wonder if they're pestered by these ants?
I catch their voices, but the words aren't clear –
her pet lip's shown itself – he's looking sulky,
murmuring secret things that I can't hear.
What's bulging in the pockets of his pants?

9.26 – he's flushed and so is she,
this could be it, although I'm not sure what!
I'm creeping nearer now, agog to see –
if that's a gun in there I might get shot!

I wonder what the heck he's up to now?
It could be double fireworks tonight!
Hang on! He's after something in her bra –
and now he's got her in a stranglehold.
Should I step in before things could go too far?
She's putting up a very feeble fight.

9.30 – time to tell them trouble's brewing –
I've got them cornered now, I'll make them pay.
I'll get the ins and outs of what they're doing,
or charge them half-a-crown to go away.

   June English

for Mary Kenny

her small feet are planted
in soft buck leather, in a cobbled street
by a red brick house she will recall
like a scene from an old film

in soft buck leather, in a cobbled street
where children hop-scotch pavements
like a scene from an old film
washing is strung like bunting

where children hop-scotch pavements
and she emerged from the womb
washing is strung like bunting
a first breath of coal-warmed air

and she emerged from the womb
she cradles her doll in a cardboard cot
a first breath of coal-warmed air
unaware she is practising

she cradles her doll in a cardboard cot
by a red brick house she will recall
unaware she is practising
her small feet are planted

Anne Kenny

I crack the crust.

A sigh of steam and I'm back, craning over the table's edge
to watch the flour-cuffed hands punching and slapping

while Uncle Frank, hair stuck to scalp, uses words
that Father says God doesn't like. I sense

a breath from the mound in the sheeted trough and spin
to check that nothing's climbing out. At the chime

of an iron catch I try not to look into the hell-fire mouth
where blue tongues stretch and reach but edge to the door,

straining to hear my mother's step on its way
to collect the warm white bag and take me home.

I watch the butter melt.

Gill Learner

Enchanter's nightshade – small white flowers.
Gone before you can whisper their name.
These are my grandmother's poison.

When the moon's half-eye is on me
and I can hear the sounds of shipwreck
ringing in the oaks, I go to the forest

and gather leaves and petals in my basket,
boil them with storm water over charcoal.
They squeak, hiss and chatter warnings.

My grandmother's flowers roar and howl
when she brews them. She pours their animal
cries into bottles. I watch her

from a distance. And when the sun
is low, evening light, she casts no shadow.

Janice Fixter

MIS/CONCEPTIONS

The moon was in fact a plateful of milk, although
nobody knew it until
the first spaceship landed with a splash.

In the overexposed sunlight of the '69 colourshot
there are actually three people
although only two can yet say 'cheese'.

Charlotte Sleigh

I was twelve, as in the twelve-bar blues, sick
for the South-East, marooned on the North Wales coast.
A crotchet, my tongue craving the music
of Welsh, Scouse, or Mancs. Entering the outpost
of Colwyn Bay pier, midsummer, noon,
nightclub for those of us with the deep ache
of adolescence, when I heard that tune,
named it in one. Soul. My heart was brake

dancing on the road to Wigan Casino,
northern soul mecca, where transatlantic bass
beat blacker than blue in glittering mono.

Then back via Southport, Rhyl, to the time, place,
I bit the Big Apple. Black, impatient, young.
A string of pips exploding on my tongue.

Patience Agbabi

THE PHOTOGRAPH

In this one I am a punk.
My hair, sprayed red, is divided
into individual fountains,
the sources of which are captured
each by a different coloured band.
Electric blue nails are painted
on the fingers of each hand,
black eye-shadow and kohl drawn around my eyes.
History Day at school. Year Six. I am ten.
A minute ago I was on time.
I don't know yet
that so many years later,
and much further down the line,
I still won't know yet.
Term Two at Uni. First Year. I am eighteen.

Victoria-Anne Bulley

Times ain't like they used to be.

Ever listen to Country?
Times have never been like they used to be.

Seriously!
Back in the day, the local palais
a kid could really stomp.
There were no fences
to our frontiers;
no collars
to fetter our breathmaking fears.
Nothing like this parent-supervised-play-date crap of today.
Be home for dinner, was all my mother had to say.
(And for dessert, she served forgiveness, rare.)

You stomp
still.
You take
a mile
and claim it
a metric inch.

(Conversion formula memorised. Please do not show all your work.)
Well, at least I never went hitchhiking.

Only because your boyfriend
was a drummer
in a punk rock band,
and drove a bedroom
in a custom van.

What's for dessert?

Shari-Lyn McArthur

The Fulham morning mist seeps stealth-cold
through the school-worn fibre of your duffle
and April cuts cruel through the card-mended soles
of your scuff-toed shoes. And you shiver, and shuffle
in the long slow queue. Ahead of you, men
stand stock still for as far as you can see
while others, still warm from recent Sunday beds,
trudge past, counting heads, hoping they won't be
too late for a Wembley seat. There since dawn,
you're used to early starts – the weekend job
on your uncle's milk float, saving all you'd earned
in a jar, till you'd made the full ten bob
for your own final ticket. But when you get home
to the gas-fired hearth and steaming hot tea,
your dad will say, 'You're far too young to go alone
to North London, in such a crowd.' So he
will take your ticket for a pound – 'That's ten bob profit!'–
and he'll go to the match in your place, in spite
of his other plans. And, on your own, you'll watch it
at home, in fuzzy nineteen-inch black and white.

Paul Curd

Friday: as usual we're playing football in the park
And I'm trying not to mark my school uniform
With tree bark and grass stains – unsuccessfully, of course.
Then talking ourselves hoarse we walk down lanes towards the shops
When one of us stops and articulates an idea:
Is there any way, do you think, perhaps, we could obtain some…
Beer? But we're

Fourteen
And at this age I have been inebriated, since my body was fated
To some early development in the facial-hair area. I have started shaving.
Which has led to some misbehaving: so now we're drinking Strongbow
With its wrong glow that's not quite orange, and not quite yellow.
Three litres three pounds though sounds like a fair price to pay to drink away
The remains of the day when you're

Fourteen
And you've already been pissed, but you've never even kissed a girl yet
And can barely tell the difference between blonde and brunette
But you know that the girl you like has hair of exquisite brown
And eyes in which you could drown and my God! Once you've heard her sing
Your heart becomes this new-made thing.
I can afford to be this foolishly romantic, a starry-eyed idiot
Not cynical or pedantic because I'm

Fourteen
And she goes away.
I send her a dozen red roses because that's what one does, one supposes:
One writes poems to express their view; gestures like that are what people do
When they're in love with a girl even though you've not shared a kiss
And if the chance did come up you're worried you'd miss...
But that's fine; there's plenty of time, because we're both

Fourteen
And love like this has never been felt by anyone ever before.
It's a new thing, I'm sure, this intensity of feeling.
It's unique, and though it leaves me reeling, I want more.
No other person could understand it: it is full of wonder and I submit that at

Fourteen
You know it all, though you've not yet had a chance to grow and fall
In love again, again… and again because being

Fourteen
It's your first taste of something as yet unfaced, a chaste memory encased
Not to be defaced, debased or displaced but to be retraced and embraced
Every time you think back to when you were

Fourteen.

Dan Simpson

i.m. Helen Penfold, 1961–1999

Things are looking up. We've
found a pub where the landlord,
convinced by my smooth lies, your

proper breasts, will serve us snakebite.
He tips the lip of each pint glass,
froths in lager, pours cider and asks

How much blackcurrant, ladies?
You smile at him, murmur *When* –
we love how his hands shake

as you take your change.
We gulp like seasoned drinkers,
avoiding the stares of the old gits

with their bitter, their racing pages.
The drink hits the spot and
everything is funny. You nearly

take my eye out playing darts.
And at the Rec on the way home,
full of sugar and gas, we slump

on the swings we dared each other
to leap from as kids, jewelling
our palms and knees with grit.

We lean back under the night sky,
under all the stars we can't name,
we're full of how we'll leave

this dump of a town first chance we get –
how we despise the regular lawns,
the sagging paddling pools, we're

singing as we approach our road.
Today was hot, like the days,
buckling with laughter, we shoved

each other over on your drive,
the tarmac sucked at our sandals
and the ice-cream van played *Lara*

from *Dr. Zhivago*, too slow. Tomorrow
we'll feel sick as dogs. But tonight,
here, under a bright, full moon,

we're amazing, and as we hug
on my doorstep, I taste you,
kiss the snakebite off your lips.

Catherine Smith

STAR-LIT

Laughing home barefoot from the disco
star-lit, care-free, safe within the pack,
high heels dangling from our hands like bracelets,
cold pavements salve dance-blistered toes,
the pulse of living sings along our blood.
We are reflected in dark High Street windows
so the night is full of us, our youth.
The cars are few, our voices own the air,
and you three boys stride out, long-limbed,
the world laid out before you for the taking,
throw back your heads, cry to the moon,
We are gods!
And I look.
And you are.

Maggie Butt

The moths were circling the flame for the seventeenth time, and you were saying how you didn't think it was that we drank too fast, just that we spoke too slow.
And that the sound of the clocks forever disagreeing was like a second heartbeat, as if the hands themselves were ageing with us.

Your tongue,
as sharp as a speechwriter's pen and twice as sincere.

Through the night we hung suspended above the clouds, with the Earth a balloon, and the ropes fraying.
We were throwing sandbags of clumsy school photographs over the side. Bailing us out.
Watching them flutter and ripple like the tired pages of small-town newspapers.
We were feeding the flames with matches made from the trees we once kissed under, and still we fell.
Tangled in the nightmares of a sea captain who fears the edge of the horizon.

Tumbling through the darkness, my stomach was a fistfight between the inertia of jet planes and the vertigo of tall buildings,
and you just smiled like a lit candle.
Lines appearing on your face as the air rushed up to meet us,
you stood calm on your worn-down high heels and said

All our lives we have been running from the vanishing point of our memories.
It is our duty to keep the pace.
We are the shadows of forgotten stars, not the dash between our dates.

Chris Moore

Smoke hangs blue and stubborn as coal dust
in the working-men's club in West Cornforth
where we girls sip gin and orange

tap purple nails on sticky tables
as brothers replay the afternoon's match
and fathers sink pints bought with women's wages.

Then the *Birdie Song*'s accordion and oompah-pah bass
call mams and nans to the parquet, a flutter of pastel Crimplene,
crests of backcombed hair dipping in the disco lights.

As the rows shuffle sideways, clap, slap hands to feet
manoeuvring within the dancefloor cage, turn repeat
keeping each other right, turn repeat, turn repeat

we girls flick our fringes, undo one more button
at the thigh of crushed-velvet midis, waiting our chance
to step out of line.

Vicky Wilson

FROZEN IN A LENS

In this one I am a flapper-dressed dancer,
One of the girls,
Our foreheads gartered with sequins and curls,
Legs lost beneath the frame's base
And Grace beaming behind.

A minute before it was nerves, glee, fear,
Excitement, practising faux-enticement,
Rushed rehearsing and lipstick searching.

I don't know yet in those pixels
The brevity of preparation's punchline.

The compere's sketch preceding us
Went on too long.

I think I missed the joke at first
But now I think I get it.

Katie Hogben

The coal shed was always scary,
A cat, a leopard, maybe a lion
Lurking in its darkness
After tea,
Chewing the nutty slack
And squeaking at my half-raised shovel

The solo walk from Sunday School
In fading dusk and pouring rain:
A giant nears, terror panics,
Tiny head atop a tall and slender horror
Silhouetted Devil coming after me
Dissolves all comic-book defiance:
Small son solemnly aloft
Upon his dad's wide shoulders,
Overcoat and trilby shared
Against the wet,
To palpitate my heart

The long route to winter football pitch
Deliberately crossing double carriageways:
Thunderous lorries bring
Brief calibrations of relief
As fiery exhausts
Defrost ice-frozen twelve year olds
Stepping nimbly into slipstreams
Leaving drivers open-mouthed

A distant cousin's wedding
And the terrifying
Vista
Of that first
Enormous dance-floor
With new and
squeaky
shoes

Hello, there

Bernard Sharratt

My mouth caked with red lipstick, imprinting
the colour like a clown's mark, a perfect kiss
on your cheek, your lips searching for mine, even
                              then I haven't told you

it'll be my first time, but we're laughing so much
on that icy beauty floor, you choosing a redder red
to paint me with so when you pull me outside
                              and I want to say

enough I can't do it, those shiny lips seal my tongue
and when we lie on your cardboard bed, thin
as those pencils waiting upright on your student desk,
                              even then

after I watch your knee nudging my thighs open,
the kiss by your crooked nose turn to a smear
of blood, even then I'm still too shy to say,
                              that was my first time,

did we do it right, the gloss still heavy on my mouth
as you laugh, lift me high above, stepping the highwire,
until I don't know, a woman now, why it mattered,
                              whatever it was I needed to say.

Sarah Salway

You taught me how to pinch the sky
and let a gap breathe through the crack,
slowly pulling apart our thumbs and fingers
to capture a person at great distance.

We peered from the beach,
saw far out to sea, chose our boats
from those that bobbed just out of reach –
mine a slimline yacht with sail ready,
yours a motorboat, fast, white.

We loosened our fingers, let the boats leave the bay
and swam out as far as the old fishing trawler.
We swept our hands along its length,
stroking the weed caught on its side;
it was soft, like a child's hair.

Abegail Morley

for Ian Jack

Lying in bed in the dark without heating. December 3rd
and feeling warm, almost too warm,
I hear the window give that rattle-burp
it only ever does when the wind is fierce outside.

Black raindrops flame on the glass. Light from across
the back gardens, one lone yellow oblong, someone
up early on a winter morning. And I think
of my parents putting radiators in their home,

dark slices of metal toast in every room. Before,
it was so cold of a morning I'd leave the next
day's clothes at the end of the bed, and I'd dress
under the blanket. Knickers, socks, vest and hand-

knitted jersey. Never without a jersey. I think of sea
current patterns explained in magazines like *National
Geographic*. Of mud slides in the Philippines
caused by the absence of tree roots

(hardwood cut down, making one illegal timber lord
happy and rich along with a Hong Kong importer;
we're a terrible short-termist lot; as Plato said,
we'll never control this except with force)

but also by the latest typhoon. Eight hundred dead
in chocolate unguent and more to be uncovered.
I think of the Gulf Stream going too much up or down
I forget which (both are bad), because the Arctic

is melting: which makes some patch of water,
crucial for the poor Gulf Stream's cycle, too hot.
Or too cold. Of how polar bears drown, hundreds
of miles from land, as ice floes under them melt.

I think of James Lovelock's face, after he'd given
his lecture explaining that most of this planet,
fifty years from now, will be underwater
beginning with Bangladesh, at the top

of the Bay of Bengal. Those tangled mangrove swamps
of Sundarbans, paradise for herons, king cobras,
honey-gatherers, fishermen, will no longer protect.
The hundred mouths of Ganges, plus sea

rising to meet the melt from Himalaya, will finally
swallow that land. All those wars, India,
Pakistan, the intricate woeful mud pie
of human history, will no longer matter

for Shiva will not be catching Ganga in his hair.
And a woman in the auditorium asks: *If all you say
is true, what should we be teaching our children?*
Now that was a question Mr Lovelock, you could see,

hadn't faced before, and his shoulders sagged.
I don't know. I really don't know. But if all
he said is true, the only answer is *commando skills.*
Fight to the death for any high ground you're standing on

my darling. I think of John Wyndham's *The Kraken
Wakes.* The window rattles again; rattles louder.
It's getting closer, faster and faster, whatever's outside,
and I know the Thames Barrier, small waters

of our particular rivers, and this terrible readiness
to worry about your own family first, may be the least
of our problems but I think *my daughter, my daughter,
how is she going to deal with this?*

Ruth Padel

only scoundrels of my caliber
can hope the seal on the lip to hamper,
can claim innocence if found to tamper
with the padlocks on the gates
which steal and siphon off great spans
of earth and planetary matter
from youth who would be their master
if only the evils of law could be undone

add to your consideration
my argument for liberation
of the spirit and the soul –
of students, whose potential
is chivvied down into mole-holes
where talent, at last, can do no good

dark abysmal pits
where the genius of the race
will not find its fit,
stifled, ambition dies
and takes with it passion,
and gratification

no loyalty at all thus remains
of life's loyal breath…

behold: nothing remains –
the sap of ascension is at large

not that my design is to simply barge
in and take away what was wrought
and fought for by our elders,
but surely some shame must fall upon those
who steal from us for lots of asphalt
the natural beauty of paradise –
I would my heart were only ice,
then my lip might bite true enough to bear
the insult of the ages
when, in finely printed schoolbook pages,
are enumerated a thousand administrative outrages
committed against the free thoughts of our patron sages
from whose wisdom in the first place
we collegians come to consider and renew,
but few are the venues that allow
our true feelings, unexpurgated, to show

Matt Moseman

Cape Town 1954–1960

In 1954
I learned that a swing
of string and bamboo
could not bear my weight.
There is a two-stitch scar on my head
to show for that lesson.

We played cricket on a short pitch
in the garden and argued
if it was 6 and out.

I learned how to make
rockets and bombs
from bangers, tins and bricks
from the local feral boy
who later tamed a squirrel
until it bit his hand,
and then made a powerful catapult
that broke windows at a distance.

Bulldozers turned our favourite
piece of waste ground
into playing fields.
Where were we going
to cook in tins
on open fires now?

Tadpoles caught
up in the woods
turned into frogs in the kitchen.

I camped in the garden
under the Southern Cross, and a fig tree.

When family friends disappeared,
legally imprisoned without charge,
we escaped by sea.

Peter Clack

Yes, darling, daddy's going the other way.
He's going to work. That's right, wave goodbye to daddy.
No, we don't have to work, we're in this queue,
With all the other boys and girls that are going to play.
No, the wagons aren't for cows and sheep.
What's the chimney for? The heating, I expect;
For the boiler, for all those showers over there.
We'll be really glad of one, won't we?
No, Gretchen won't need a shower, she's just a dolly;
So is Gerda, but we just had to leave her behind in all the hurry.

Yes, Uncle Reuben came last month.
I expect he was too busy settling in to send us a postcard.
No, he won't have been working: he's too old, darling.
Yes, I expect we'll be meeting him soon.
And who knows? Daddy might join us too, when he's too tired to work.
Let's sing a little song now: no, not the one about Hansel and Gretel.
Hold tight to Mummy, Esther; Mummy won't say your name again.

Graham Anderson

I wake and see and love the sun-dust,
trembling every morning in the brightness
coming through the hole in the wall.
mama smiles, and she is trying
very hard to be happy again,
starting, as she says, from the outside –
where smiles collect sometimes
on her red-eyed wrinkly face
like friendly patches stuck on
by the good old sun.

Those who have gone away we must think of
as heroes. Daddy went away so quickly
when the quick thunder entered
through the wall… A fire-demon
casting its flashing spell threw me,
like my dolly, under the table –
perhaps to play with later…
But look, I am a good girl now,
and when Mama says
I'll see Daddy again one day

I can be brave, believe, smile, and say yes.

Alan Gleave

But we didn't have snow,
I can't remember that.
Nor tank-tracks, frozen grey,
smeared with blood;
the swaddled women,
carrying buckets
backwards and forwards,
indecipherable;
the soldiers firing
at windows.

I remember running –
a sudden silence
broken. And a crater
between houses in a garden,
after the All-Clear,
I remember that.
And later, at school,
the two empty desks.

Geraldine Paine

Fingers, feet, vertebrae. I count them all
into this body – it's down to numbers.
I close my eyes, imprint form and flesh
past the curve of you.
It's been weeks since I've seen the ground
as my belly stretched to fit the way you curl yourself around,
swell to fill me, with the angles of your limbs
projecting through my skin. I felt you
grow, divide, survive. I'm
sculpting you with each breath, willing every cell:
one two three four.
My hands and I count
pulses through skin, resonating with
heartbeats – yours
shakes me at the edge of sleep. I'm split by
your violent arrival.

Your violent arrival
shakes me. At the edge of sleep I'm split by
heartbeats, yours
pulses through skin, resonating with
my hands. And I count
one two three four,
sculpting you with each breath, willing every cell
grow, divide, survive. I'm
projecting through my skin – I felt you
swell to fill me with the angles of your limbs
as my belly stretched to fit. The way you curl yourself around
it's been weeks since I've seen the ground
past the curve of you.
I close my eyes, imprint form and flesh
into this body. It's down to numbers:
fingers, feet, vertebrae – I count them all.

Nicky Gould

*Doctors in the Iraqi city of Fallujah are reporting a high level of birth defects, with some
blaming weapons used by the US after the Iraq invasion. (BBC News 4 March 2010)*

Just after the big bang particles and antiparticles repeatedly annihilated each other in bursts of energy, which in turn created more particles, and so on; but this process ended with very slightly more matter than antimatter, making the universe possible.

Arriving at the church for the children's charity concert
we remembered the words of Richard Feynman:
Created and annihilated,
created and annihilated –
what a waste of time.
He was speaking of those particles and antiparticles
at the beginning of time
annihilated in explosions of light.

In the church the children were playing
for the refugees of Kosovo;
our granddaughter's long hair shone
like the sheen of her violin.
She did not know
she was a child of that hair's breadth victory
of particles over antiparticles
in the early universe: annihilation
for all but a few, a final imbalance
just enough for making galaxies and worlds
and at that end of time
those children and the making of their years.

They played Bach and *Twinkle twinkle little star,*
not knowing what a star is
or the violence of stars,
not knowing they were perfected children
of the violent universe,
not knowing the years piled up on the scrap heaps
of that country they'd raised money for...
the man with his ear sawn off slowly
and fed to a dog like offal, the girl
with her legs torn off, her family machine gunned,
blown into darkness.

So many annihilations of perfected years.
But also those children in their panache of light.

Daphne Gloag

When you come, dear Sponsor,
I say, *Karibu from Mercy Wambui!*
We sit spooning Mum's groundnut soup.
Asante, I say, *for good job you do*
assisting me in school fees.
Mother's happy you volunteer
so I can excel in life.

When you come,
we walk by Thika's river,
climb together to Fourteen Falls.
You buy Maasai blanket to sleep in.
I ask why you help me,
you say, *Service to mankind*
is service to God.

When you come,
I tell you my story –
that father leave us,
school is hard when I'm hungry.
You listen how rain don't come,
people we know die
because livestock become bone.

When you come,
Asante for ribbons and bookmark.
Not say Mum sell pens you send,
no talk of goat you pay for die.
I fear if my school marks be bad
you no longer sponsor. But in photo,
you have kind teacher look.

When you come,
I appreciate golden opportunity
God gives me to speak in the face.
Tell you I think my mother afraid
you take me away from her,
'to fulfil my ambitions'
and she have no help on farm.

But you never come, Mum say.
I think she right that I dream –
better that way. Dear Sponsor,
may God enlarge borders for you.

Margaret Eddershaw

In Kiswahili karibu = welcome; asante = thanks

The girls spat at me, frothing like hyenas,
shouting, '*kintirleey*'. They rubbed mud
into my face telling me I was dirty
but I was wearing a crisp white shirt.
At home I cried and my grandmother sent cold
looks to Mama.

Mama went back to our old village to stay
while my auntie had her baby. Our new house
lost its dance and song. My grandmother
smiled like a crocodile. I felt sad. I felt naked
to the eyes of her sisters and cousins whispering
on the courtyard steps.

My first term of school ended. I woke to voices
chanting. My grandmother fetched me
telling me this was a special day,
telling me that the other girls would like me now,
telling me that the dirty thing that grew between my legs
was going to be taken away.

In her room there was a table with a clean white cloth.
There were lots of aunties and a man with a mole on his chin
and a gold front tooth. They told me to lay on the table.
My grandmother leaned across my chest and held me down.
Her breath was sweet as she moved across my face to whisper,
'the *kintir* will be removed now'.

Two of them take off my panties and hold my legs out far apart.
I can't breathe enough to let out the scream sitting in my throat.
The man takes a pair of scissors from his bag and pulls my skin
down there. I feel sick. My body explodes into my head. I'm dying.
I wake and shake, see blood and shake, pee a burning fire
and die again.

They sew me up like a football.
They tie my legs together.
My grandmother grows soft during the days
she tends to my wounds. She hums and washes me
telling me to be very still. She smiles and strokes my forehead
telling me, 'You are pure now.'

Maggie Yaxley Smith

VI

It was a high red dome
of cloth, black-spotted, some kind of bug –
a ladybird –
                    and she stood beneath it speechless,
pink in its reflected glow.

The two white crescents of its eyes
were two white flags on a billow of red sail

or pennants fluttering slowly down
through layers of grey air

to land her safely here at the glass door.

Is there any way to write about her?
Something I hardly know

clutches and opens,
                    starts to run warm
and I shut it off.

                    But isn't it possible
to see a red umbrella over a tiny girl
and think of – what?
                    -- the *oh*, the *ah*,
the *yes* of it, the laugh

that's something like hope?
                        At her side her father
touches her small elbow
and smiles, seeing my face. He nudges her gently

gently forward, under the collapsing ribs.

   Susan Wicks

You took your time coming. It's 44 degrees
in the Blue Mountains, Eucalyptus explodes
as you struggle up and down your mum's stomach,
banging on her heart, one thumb in the mouth,
ignoring ultrasounds and alarmed academics,
irresponsibly kicking the placenta to one side,
enlarging the liquor-dome till she can't walk,
cannoning hormones, borrowing her oxygen.

And we were up on the snowy side of the planet
waiting for the sun's penumbra to shift to Spring,
until that morning we saw a black swan on the lake
and I knew you'd come out yawning and calling,
the exception that would not be put off, one of
those things you rely on when the world seems stuck.
You'd opened your eyes. Another explosion.

Roger James

SHATTER

trying times – a child's
cry claims mind, body; my own
tears as molten glass

CRADLE CALL

the manchild cries out
for me in the night, my lap
his damp curls' cradle

Natalie Savage

I may have thought how strange it was
that the sister I used to balance
on hands and feet for acrobatic shows
in the lounge, the little girl
who used to dance on the wide ledge
of the bedroom window with next door's boys,
was now spread out on this trestle,
her swollen sex every shade of maroon.

But when the flamboyant red parted
like a vertical lid and the blind white crown
of my niece appeared, when she lay
between my sister's slack knees,
bluish and floury, her cry as mundane
and miraculous as you could wish,

and when I watched the midwife draw down
the perfect lobes of the placenta
with its marbled cord, exotic as a water lily,
for that moment I understood everything
and the world hung ripe in my reach.

Sue Rose

EMMIE

Sitting in the marquee, daddy, mummy
and I were watching Indian women dance.
Their silky costumes sparkled red and bold,
henna weaving through their long black hair,
a dot of gold nestled above their eyes.
You seemed happy on your daddy's lap.
Then you looked up at me, reached out, crawled
from his knee to mine. You straddled my leg.
I smiled and was thrilled when you tugged
my hair and ears. Then soon you sat there still.
Dancers' hands and arms were swirling, twirling,
bare feet tap tapping the wooden floor,
bells around their ankles ringing, singing.
My kisses swam among your creamy curls.

Amal Garnham

for Ffion b. 7 April 2005

What is
this tender catch,
this fresh spill of creases
and folds, small miracles of nails?

What is
this swell and heave
of laundry, old clocks struck
dumb, nights now trickling towards dawn?

And this –
your hearts adrift
with a ripple of breath
in her throat, the tug of her lips.

She's sea
flooding the plains
of your lives. Every day
it deepens – you can hardly breathe.

Lynne Rees

HALF SHELL FOR MOLLY

A curled piece of butter. One petal. Tiny seahorse mouth poking out.

It's the worked dough in a soft roll you might be making, or a fancy biscuit.
The shape of your grown-up thumb along one side, where you might press.

It's the insides of things. The beautiful what's-left. The palest coral blush. What
you might have slipped into your pocket at nursery: torn off wool, acorn hat,
worn stick.

The part of you that protects. And is protected.

Patricia Debney

My daughter taught me
gravity in the bath.
It's something we can't live
without she said – or chickens
would fly
though they already fly she
pointed out
when men don't clip their wings.
I thought of how I'd wanted to
silence her
and wondered if she was
listening.
And if men don't clip their
wings
then geese can fly too.
But we don't want to catch our
dinner with a net
and she
chuckled.
What would be the point I said
of bringing her down.
And I hoped she didn't listen.

Then she laid her head on
my wet body and closed her
eyes.
I thought of saying
Don't
don't you do that
or you might drown.
But I didn't.

Lorraine Kashdan-Lougher

Late and quiet with all my keys
for the door, I hope you've not
yet been laid in your cot,
but find in the bathroom
a tubful of water, empty, well-
used and barely lukewarm

and to tell you the truth,
there's the earth of my regret,
the little warmth the water
has, its tiny fractions
stolen from your playful heat

how it shows I've come too late
for the intimacy
of your straight-backed body
cut at the waist by cooling water,
those few gallons of sudsy wash
that cooled that much more slowly
for you being there

that now I let go, stir away
with both hands, think something
obvious, grasping what is gone.

Martyn Crucefix

Wide-eyed to the camera, beautiful always,
A water-melon grin in a pirate hat,
Or daisy-chained, down daisy-chains of days,

Wraiths of your children. There, with a yoghurt pot,
A spoon and a shovelling hand, the baby showed
How, in between times, babies laugh a lot,

And her sister in her wellies has a toad
She kisses into metamorphosis.
No! Any road, she'd rather have a toad.

But last, most beautiful and most rare, is this:
Both of them on the back step, so intent
On mud blancmange or centipede, they miss

The shutter's click. You wonder what it meant,
Such protean brightness falling from the air,
The honeysuckle sprawled improvident,

Withered long since. And you not there. Not there.

John Whitworth

ROSA

It's a wonder no one crushed
its soundless open beak,
or inadvertently put out its eyes
under a passing wheel.
Tattered in the gutter
that pigeon was nothing but an object lesson
on the kindness of death.

Your school bag, falling forward,
nearly dealt its lolling head another blow
as you slid pages torn from Tolkien under it,
making a cradle out of elven spells
in which to warm it in your hands.
Believing in the power of names,
you called it Rosa. Rosa, Rosa

Moyra Tourlamain

Too early to discard the primary-school uniform,
you contented yourself with choking Teddy
with your winter-green tie. Poor thing, looked
quite startled with his solitary popped eye.

And you were in the bathroom singing
the latest Spice Girls' song while I
sorted and packed a box for the loft:
Peter Rabbit, Ladybirds, Colouring In.

A new moon spied me, through the pane,
white as bone but for one red streak
which would bring you running back,
bewildered to my arms.

Maureen Jivani

NEW YEAR SONNET

My father, bending, taught me skimming stones.
A beach like this, tossed and wild with bluster,
Black rags of crow hang in the pewter sky.
Flat, grey and spinning, the pebbles skip and,
Kissing liquid lead, they leave behind an
Ever diminishing osculation.
Surface tension; memory bounces off
The water's plane, his fingers on my arm,
The grip too hard, checking my abandon.
Now, my daughter is tugging at my arm,
'A sixer mum!' she's laughing, staggering
 As her hoard of wave-worn stones bags out her skirt.
'I can do it.' Braced, she shrugs me away,
And whips her skipping flint across the brine.

Jane Francis

Back and forth, back and forth
he sweeps across the window of my mind
A small figure running earnestly
pushing before it a red broom just his height
sweeping the kitchen floor.

The front porch covered in leaves:
at last a task and tool within his ken.
The yard broom twice his height
collects a satisfying pile of autumn leaves –
over the edge he sweeps them
but cannot manipulate the broom's head back up.

With a tablespoon from a huge mixing bowl he offers me food
the way I feed him from a Bunnykins bowl with a teaspoon.

The new Iris Murdoch purloined from the coffee table
taken to his own small sofa – deep in concentration he turns the pages.

Playing quietly on the floor suddenly he's up,
runs to the laundry and returns nappy in hand
presses then rubs the carpet vigorously.
Yes, he has wet the floor but he has also mopped it up.

Once he has mastered ascending the kitchen chairs
his high chair declines in importance
reduced to part of a climbing frame.
Real people sit at the table to eat.

Toys? What do real people do with toys?
They collect them and put them into containers
so, so do I – over and over again.

How do adults behave? What do real people do?
Well look – I can do it too!

Virginia Lowe

She's first, the only one
who's never climbed before, not fluent
in the language of the climb,

stumbling over words she needs
to understand ascent. What still voice whispers
Choose this handhold, place your foot here

as the cliff rises sheer above her?
The sun glints off the rock face like a knife's edge.
Unfazed, she changes feet, grips hard

with two small hands. Below,
the man with the belay rope
looks calmly on; it creaks and slips in the piton

as she steps up and up towards the top,
turns to wave, then leans away from safety,
bracing steady feet against the cliff. Anchored

to the rock face, she abseils down to meet us.
Mum, Dad, that was so cool!
You looked so small!

How will we, left holding clothes
she'll soon outgrow, adjust our step
to this new child?

Vivienne Tregenza

For Freddie, after several years of school runs,
a total distance the equivalent of circling the Earth

Side by side through green sub-tropics, temperate drizzle,
thunder, early dark – twenty-five thousand miles –
we knew where we were heading. We tried
to take the right kit (thermal vests and Wellingtons
are an embarrassment crossing the Nullarbor Plain).
Sunny days we wore hats, not in snow – you
loved to lower the window, thrust your bare head out,
feel crystals prickle your ears and nose. We stalled
near the South Pole; shivering in grey Terylene
you crunched over ridges of ice to plant a flag.
That June we bumped through Amazon rainforest,
paintbox parakeets feathered the windscreen, anacondas
slid beneath the bumpers when we stopped
to put Brazilian air in our tyres. One blue-gold autumn
we told knock-knock jokes across the Sahara, we wintered
along the Nile playing hide-and-seek with pyramids and stars.
And when we forgot compass, calculator, maps,
your sense of direction kept us on track. From Moscow to Paris
you counted four hundred and sixty-two onion domes,
eleven hundred smoking chimney-stacks. In Tibet you said,
Let's stay. I like temples, turmeric, Himalayas. But we drove on –
that's what we did. There's time to go round again,
but you tell me your passport photo is out of date,
you're nine now, not six, or seven, or eight.

Clare Best

for my grandson Kieren (14.2.2001) and my grandmother Angie Brazh
(14.2.1898–6.8.1973)

Were you to meet, what would you say?
Between your birthdays more than a hundred years
Five generations, and the Atlantic Ocean
Between her Guyana and your England.

Would you call her Mother, like we all did?
Rushing to meet her over the bridge
The donkey cart waiting as she paid the driver
Four grand-daughters ecstatic at her arrival?

Would she have travelled along the Corentyne Highway?
Or sailed downriver from Kwakwani?
Would she have brought her parrot, her Polly
Or naughty Jack, the capuchin monkey?

I can see you now scrambling for her lap
With your Bob the Builder truck and your Scoobydoo top
And you'd chatter about Shrek and your new DVD
And your Game Boy and what's on the telly

And she'd stroke your blond hair, admire
Your blue eyes, say was a blessing, a St Valentine child
A boy child, after all these girls, but who
Was Scoobydoo and what was telly?

And she might ask who you were named for, St Kieren?
And how she so proud your Mummy name Eloise
Like her sister Eloise and did you know the name Brazh was Portuguese?
Her family come from Madeira, you know!

You think is co-incidence the two of y'all
Share the same birthday? And she'd press a gold piece
In your hand and say

No matter how big the world, wide the sea
No matter even a thousand years pass
Family was family.
Happy Birthday Valentine boy.

Maggie Harris

                                    The

                 Sea
                                 Silent

                                 She
                              Wanted
                My childhood to return

Seahorses
                           Never to be
                           Saddled

           silent lotus

She carried me inside her
She carried me on her shoulder
She carried me as I grew
Gradually bolder
She carried me.

We were part of one body
I nestled at her heart
Until our bodies
Sweetly fell apart
Then we were two bodies.

The first words I heard
Were her low croon,
She gazed at my cradle
Like the full moon
And her language was milk.

She called me by name
Not Tom, Dick or Harry,
Her words in mine
Are the words that I carry
And all day she calls me.

Carrying it seems
Is what we must do.
You carried me mother
As I carry you
As we carry each other.

George Szirtes

Picture this:
A room.
A window.
Yellow walls.

In the foreground
Still life at a table:
A forearm supine;
An elbow upright with a cup.
A pose of drinking:
An empty cup;
An ordered smile.

I remember!

My mind needles it, this
Frieze of play-back
Memory becoming mnemosyne.

My father.
I am in the picture with
This thought:
To hold my cup just so as he.
You can see me looking at him
Looking at the camera
And see I haven't got
Quite the hang of it
To look just like my father
With the cup below his upper lip
I cannot do
Because my chin is just above the table
And the cup is swallowing my head
And my two eyes are looking
Just to see if I am looking
Sort of casual and relaxed
And you can tell from this I wasn't
With my head inside the cup.

I remember I was thinking that.
Never did quite get his measure.
But who was it took that picture?
Must have been my mother, I suppose.

Karl Birjukov

When, night after night, the siren wailing,
my mother said, 'All right now'
to her little girls, five, four and two,
downstairs in the double bed,
and 'Go to sleep now',
we closed our eyes.

When my father, the air raid warden, went out,
my mother embroidered the tablecloth I've kept,
or knitted dolls' clothes, or smoked cigarettes
as she read the *Daily Express*.

When she sat up nights with my father
till the 'All Clear', playing cards, drinking tea,
she made dripping sandwiches
with onions sliced thin to transparency.

When the bomb blew the windows in
and glass scattered over us in the bed,
my father burst in to gather up
his screaming little girls in wet nighties.

When we had been given apples and warm bread,
we stood by the front door as the milkman called
as usual for the jug to take milk from the churn,
and we watched as our mother skirted the crater
to where the milkman's horse was waiting
for apple cores and her soft words.

Felicity Brookesmith

Family holidays started at three a.m.,
loaded in blankets into a black Minx,
sleeping through empty London, heading west.

Detours to have a picnic, stretch our legs.
Meeting a coach in high-hedged, narrow lanes.
The last few miles. Arrival. Exploration.

All taken care of. All done for us children.
One summer it rained the whole time. Cooped up
indoors we fought and squabbled constantly.

Near the end my mother dropped a glass jug.
The word *Damn* broke from her lips, first time
we'd ever heard her swear. It left us speechless.

All that pent up force. All that loss of face.
The word filled the room, had to be ignored –
as if the jug, smashed, had at once re-formed,

continued to serve, dared us to notice.

Mark Roper

spent her pocket-money
on bottles of Corona with flip tops,
gob-stoppers, black jacks,
aniseed balls. Shared it all.

I hoarded my money
in a small tin letter-box
ha'penny by ha'penny
and counted it daily.

My doggy hot-water-bottle
was called Pouncey.
My sister's was a rabbit
called Theophilus.

My sister sewed miniature clothes
for my dolls, stood me
in a washing-up bowl
as a candle
with crepe-paper flame
while she, moth-winged,
danced round me.

She was too clever
for me. At times I'd flip,
pummel her forehead with my fists
through clenched teeth bleating
gdjah! gdjah!

   Jenifer Kahawatte

Six weeks, two full teaspoons
of syrupy pinkness, morning, noon, night,
and my mother would dry
her hands on her skirt, perch,
silent, just till she hoped
she'd seen me swallow, then go.

And in between, there was
sleeping and waking and making
wallpaper shapes turn into bears,
hoping they'd be the gentle,
honey-bearing sort.

And every evening, Dad would come
and sit next to me, and we'd watch
old gangster films, Noggin the Nog, the Dickens
serial. *More Daddy, more.*

And he'd teach me stuff like –
twende baharini – which means, perhaps,
let's go to the sea, in Swahili.
When you're better, he'd say. *When
you've had all that medicine,
and you're better.*

Then he'd be quiet again, and stay
till the bears went home.

Simone Mansell Broome

RED CROSS

It was good that dad was a first aider
Because every time my nose bled
I knew to lay on the kitchen floor
And let him finish reading the newspaper.

Ted Smith-Orr

My mum would look out of the kitchen window
on a bleak summer's day and say,
'Of course we'll go to the beach. It'll be fine soon',
as we stood shivering in sun-dresses,
clutching rubber rings and bathing hats.

Undaunted, ignoring the sound of beating rain
on the coal shed, mum poured tea into a flask
and made up bottles of orange squash.
When the picnic was ready, the sun came out and stayed.
Mum never let us down.

Wrapped in a towel, after a swim, we ate sliced white bread
from the Co-op, filled with sliced tomatoes and dollops
of salad cream. Mum was magic.
The sun always shone when she was around.

Hilary Drapper

HOLDING MOTHER'S HAND

As a wayward village boy I shunned
My mother's hand as she tried
To guide me across the busy High Street.

Visits to town were usually punctuated
By mother scolding me for my early
Search for independence and self-expression.
Sobbing and sniffles added to my embarrassment
Of mother making a fool of herself.

Now a middle-aged, slightly wiser boy
Holds his aged mother's hand as she negotiates
Pavement cracks and kerbstones
On the way home in the dark.

'It's no good getting older if you don't get wiser,'
Mum used to say.

Harry Harris

Yards of woven raw cotton
are scrunch-cut into pieces
like the jigsaw that I fashion
sitting on the veranda,
shaded from afternoon sun,
its glare as piercing as pins
pricking with every turn.
I listen to the rhythmic hum –
Is it done, is it done?

A pattern has to be followed,
clothes made for changing bodies,
the hems allow for growth.
Pieces are put together,
by endless fitting and matching.
The picture gradually forming,
the handle keeps on turning –
Nearly done, nearly done.

A dress is ready for wearing,
buttons and belt sewn on.
I dance about the veranda
pleased with the way I look.
The jigsaw is completed
and proudly shown to all.
Now they are boxed in a cupboard –
All done, all done.

Patricia Griffin

Hiroshige, '26 Nissaka', from 'The 53 Stations of the Tokaido' (print)

She follows the road, it lists above bamboo,
tea plantations, mist and blue mountains.

Every stone covered in moss,
left-over rain drips,
pools. Knit one
purl one. Smell of rotting.

Sound of branches breaking
in the wood dense with cryptomeria
dark as woad.

> *Who's there?*

Thwack of blade
and blood scythes
from the wound, black rain
streams, covers
tree and stone.

Bamboo and tea trees witness
a birth and a death,
say nothing.

An owl with one eye open
sighs, heads fall.

> *I am wanting to speak to my mother*
> *but my mother is dead.*

The hills sag in bewilderment.

> *I am looking for my mother*
> *but she has disappeared.*
> *I mourn my mother*
> *from the day I am born.*

Nancy Gaffield

The print's subtitle is 'Sayo amid the mountains'. The legend tells of a birth at night.
At this spot a robber attacked and killed a pregnant woman who had stopped to rest against
a stone. A passing Buddhist monk rescued the newborn child. Years later, the murderer took
his sword to be mended, boasting to the swordsmith about how he had killed the woman and
damaged his sword. The swordsmith, the murdered woman's son, took his revenge. The ghost
of the woman lives in the stone; it wails each night.

Boys stoned frogs the summer my father died,
surrounded the stream, there was never any hope,
and followed the floating white bellies.

My sister and I were left there, in Accord, New York,
in a bungalow swarming with cousins.
We wanted to be like them, unaware

of our steps as we ran through the dark grass.
Or of night's enormity – all those beautiful stars
forgotten above the wooden roofs.

Our aunts lived windows apart
and our uncles wore those white undershirts
with the scooped-out neck and arms.

On porch steps, as the orange light collected moths,
Aunt Dorothy kissed us goodbye, unable to answer
questions we couldn't ask.

At home, lilacs and roses still bloomed under my window.
Nose pressed against the screen, I longed to hear
my parents' voices murmuring in the garden.

Mara Bergman

My grandfather is *lying down* in the front room
with the curtains drawn but I'm not allowed to pry.
Nor can I wonder why the door is locked,
or whether he will ever wake up.

Even that day when the roof caved in at the pit,
he was sitting up for Sunday dinner by two.
Just got held up at work for a bit.

It's the first time he hasn't carved the beef
since he *served his country* and the question
I want to ask him – about why some people die
and others *fall asleep* – will have to wait.

  John Mackay

GREAT-GRANDAD

Great-Grandad Morgan was tall –
a Nick Drake type of tall.
He spoke from his throat, his mouth
a scissure, a rented malaise of
deep hums, which

I struggled to understand, yet
sat by his long knees, as he
sat by himself, occasionally
patting me like a dog or a thought

he'd perhaps lost, then found again.
Hours would go by, him humming,
me waging war with pegs and
pipe-cleaners, in and around
his immaculate brogues

that he kept by his feet
always 'toosore' for hell
or for leather.

  Kris Thain

April
and already they're selling sweet peas
small, wickedly expensive bunches
flounce of anaemic petticoats

I walk again
into a shadowed hall
shiver of house cool against outside heat
am transfixed
by the fire he's lit in the gloom
blaze of magenta and maroon
leavening the lesser pastel shades
the sharp-sweet
one-note fragrance dancing on wax polish
tobacco, the safe composty smell of him

purblind after bright sun
I see his fingers rough from working
gritty Cheshire sandstone soil
the dirt etching their cracks and folds
imagine them cutting wiry stems
patiently settling the blooms to this riot of colour

and two skinny girls
nurtured like plants
the three of us playing house
fishing for sticklebacks, flying on swings

together tending long avenues of sweet pea

Marilyn Donovan

for Granddad King

Have I told you...?
And our world lights up
From your glinting spectacles
To eyebrows lifted in laughter
Wiggling into animation

Fine hairs becoming intricate
Details
Of a mosquito you caught
Or the hundred crooked crossroads
Down the Khyber Pass.

And yes it is remarkable that
The chocolate wrapper told me
The answer all those years ago,
Its *Crepuscule*
Perfectly counterpointed by
The dawning on your face
Of a joy that awoke
The child in us both.

So when these days of yours
Are drawing to a close
And still that glimmer shines
Through eyes
Cataracted over
Through a face
Clouded with age

I'll carve each story into the wrinkles
Growing round my smiling eyes,
And promise I'll never tell you that
You've told me this before.

Becky King

He pulls plastic cups from the cupboard –
yellow   green   orange   pink
one white bowl

arranges them on the table   all upside down
some near me   some far away
He tells me to hold the yellow one still
in the centre

His calloused hands spin the cups slowly
turn them round and round my yellow one

These are the planets   he says
you hold the sun

In the dim light there are no stars yet
colours take on the shape of spheres
this white bowl the moon

and it is hard for me to hold the sun
I want to spin away   draw figure-eights
around earth and moon

I don't yet know someone has already walked there
don't know about light years or the milky way

Long after I leave the table   he keeps spinning them
rotating worlds in sequences

  until all the patterns make sense
   until the universe comes alive

 Liz Bahs

Here is a skein of wool, three ply
and softly speckled with pale grey.
I love it when you start knitting.
Tongues of flame crackle among sticks
leaping in and out of each other
to lick the soot from the chimney.
Naples yellow tiles of the fireplace
climb in steps to the mantelpiece.
Each ledge has its own treasure: a pebble
from Lancing, a miniature photo,
a cobalt wing in a butterfly brooch.
You undo your skein of wool,
I place my hands facing, a foot apart.
You put the loop of the skein between
my thumbs and palms. You take the loose end
and begin to wind round the fingers
of your left hand – the hand with the Welsh gold ring.
Now you wind in the other direction
and slowly a ball begins to take shape.
Stems, leaves and chrysanthenum heads
gaze from their orderly cretonne design
on the arm of your chair.
I sway my arms from right to left
then left to right in easy rhythm,
like a snake in slow motion
making figures of eight,
to ease the progress of the thread
flowing from me to you, circling its way
on to the growing globe.

Geraldine Cousins

Grandmother, coaxed from her Krakow village
to where Coca-Cola signs blinked red-and-white
against the night sky,
told me of Joseph and his coat of many colours
in a language I never learnt but somehow always knew.

Grandfather, who left the wrinkled roads of his städtel
for the car-honking world that rushed so heedlessly by him,
sometimes allowed me to sit on his knee.

Father, a man of dreams I never knew, warmed my little feet
in his bed when icicled Sunday mornings frosted our windows
so we couldn't see neighbours who were unlike us.

Mother spoke to me of the girl she was in her village
to the boy I can no longer be.

My parents left all they knew, stepped from steerage
onto the not-so-golden streets of a 'Promised Land'
where they made me one hot and sweaty tenement night,
and gave me a childhood not so much lost
as displaced from somewhere I'd never been.

Fred Bazler

my uncle
bes boatman in de world
hold oars like dey his arms

mammy say he don need oars
row good wid de hands

my uncle
make sail fill even if dere no wind
move boat through water
like big fish after guppies

mammy say he don need boat
he swim good as stingray

my uncle
catch crawfish wid old harpoon
bite head off electric eels
open beer bottles
wid de teeth

mammy
I say
how come he bite so well?

mammy finger her throat
say he ought be born barracuda
god make dreadful mistake

    Caroline Carver

1
He observed men building houses:
how they cleared ground
for digging to bed-rock.

He watched them balancing,
with the body's knowledge,
pillatrees on steep slopes.

He marvelled at the way
things came together with intimacy
of halving joints, mortise and tenon,
constructing a logic men live by.

For a long time he stood beneath immortelles
in awe with corn birds weaving hanging nests;
he knew then it would take a life-time
of ingenuity to build the house
he wished to grow wise in.

2
It was hard work digging a pit of clay,
dancing in the straw with bare feet,
pugging mortar to shape rooms to his desire.

As he danced, he dreamed of moulding
a room around silence, a place in which to foetal-curl,
suspend thoughts of how to survive;
another, without corners,
walls smoothed to a mirror
with the friction of love.

He danced dreaming
of the one where he would store
the things he had given power to:
an owl's mummified wing,
his navel string, never planted,
withered like a dead yam vine;
the cosmic pebble, like a bull's black eye
that almost struck his father down.

The last room was for his mother.
She died when he was nine.

John Lyons

One year my brothers made a mask; a present for my sister.
I was terrified of the dancing eyes that moved behind
the papier-mâché face,
and wouldn't let her wear it.

Yet hidden in the box room, even when the door was only left ajar,
it terrified me in a way I'm certain Father Christmas was not supposed to do.

Rooms seemed endless, where names alone could conjure up
the dusty cobwebs of their shadowy-ness:
that box room with its mask; the walk-in pantry, with its huge and
    rumbling fridge;

the strange perspective of the torch-lit under-stairs;
the locked and curtained summer house;

a coal-dark shed with its glistening heaps;
the outside loo's thoughtful separateness;
the damp and dusty, window-lit apple shed, full of ancient tools and
    apple trays;

the bike shed, where I had my little bench and set of Christmas tools;
the stable block where, up a ladder, a trapdoor hid an old stage sword;

a disused pigsty, beyond the apple trees and vegetables,
a mummified cat squashed between a stack of doors;

and last but not least, the rusty, lock-up garages,
where the magic shapes of motor cars were kept.

Each secret world, an atmosphere of strange dumb things,
which simply lay forgotten, with no one watching them;
dreaming doors, so full of mystery that imagining awoke and tip-toed in.

And then there were those eyes, and more illusive fears,
revealed in the shadowy forms of dressing gowns on bedroom doors;
and the, not unpleasant, nor un-natural, sense of presence on the turning
    of the stair,

that little landing where the books were kept.

Phil Barrett

Probably even now, or even in my sleep,
I could walk that route, the echo of earlier feet

shadowing of my younger self, as dutiful
I trod the street, across the road, through the gate

(that's labelled 'please keep closed')
along beneath the big trees in the park, noting

one with wrought-iron fencing embedded in the bark
and the other which is a giant's hand (disguised)

then turning up the hill across more roads and past
where the cinema has not reopened

even to this day (and rivals, from out of town,
now keep it that way) and thence into that long stretch

of alleys, climbing across the hill, almost secret
in the way they hardly touch the roads, past St Mary's

and the post office, the fire station, that funny
little shop, just opposite the car showroom where

now at last, the journey starts to drop and slow
as I lope slowly down the longish stately road

that slopes down to school and another gate.
And where my English homework is very, very late.

Ian Badcoe

With her ornate feet
and wrought-iron hair,
Mrs McIntyre shouts, you swim.

Head up, draw breath,
glimpse the gallery spectators,
shy and dry, and plunge, slip,

breathe through your gills,
look through your portholes.
The boat rocks and plunges

on another round-the-world voyage.
Forty-nine laps and fifty-one to go.
Feet wrinkled into fins

and up round along,
down round along
and again. Go!

Oh derelict memory. Your gunnels
and runnels all intact,
but where do you pay your money?

Empty it out. Swill the tiles
and bolt the doors.

Go home, with your ponytail dripping
down your school shirt-back
and your fish and chips.

It's the Wednesday-night wriggle,
all bottoms and feet and knickers
and goggles. Your bobble's dead,

flat, in a pool of chlorine and urine.
Don't bend or they'll see your bum.

Lucy Rutter

I didn't care much for the axolotls,
primitive salamanders which like newts
develop from gilled larvae into adults
but often don't mature to adult shape,
some never getting past their tadpole stage
(Daddy's pet parable for use in schools).
The dozing python curled inside its cage
was duller than its name, the electric eels
could neither shock nor thrill behind their glass,

unlike the ranks of horned or antlered skulls
and white, articulated skeleton
towering above us, of the giant Bone
Elephant with his curving ivory tusks,
rigid as Aaron's serpent, smooth and still.

Janet Montefiore

HOBHEY WOOD

Fingertips glide over burnished wheat blades.

Pulled leaves fly above hedgerows and thickets
and boggy water mud puddles.

Speckled, dappled, spotted lights sprinkle.
Reflections dart.

Rusty, yellow leaves smush into sodden ground.

Sunlight warms your face. Makes you glow.

The weathered tether-rope swing hangs
stagnant over mud dunes.

Twisted, writhing branches set in embrace.

Ice-cold water soothes and freezes,
curving worn-round pebbles on your soles.

The thorn in your fleshy heel.

The dirt under your fingernails.

Miranda Dobson

Smells are the ghosts of past times, the shorthand
of the mind, recalling memories as
sharp as frosty evenings under stars:
tar melting on the roadway of childhood's
long summer twilights; lavender sickly
in grandmother's room; spicy buns in a
cinnamon kitchen; burnt porridge and
babyshit in the back room of our lodgers.

I slavered at the ravenous roast on
Sunday lunchtimes in the radio warmth:
at the leathery punch of my father's cobbling struggle
to keep soles sound and sinless for playground football,
like the red ball in the green sweet
cricket pitch of the new-cut season.
On sultry nights the sour reek of the river,
effluvia of summer heat, carried
seawards, to war skies, where the woodsmoke
of bonfire night blackened into bombsites
and mildewed farms. The old sow putrefied,
combusted in corrupted ferns, and ether
ended childhood in a-rheumatic fever.

Derek Score

We children are included, are swept up
in the harvest's wild sea. Men sweat and shout
pitch up the golden wheat. Our one desire
to ride the piled wagons, dipping galleons.
We hang beneath, black with the axle grease.
Strictly forbidden to ride, we wonder
watch and will the huge horse leg by leg
straining to start the treasure up the hill
hedges snatch handfuls as it squeezes by.

I buy a ticket for a carriage ride
the wheels have tyres this time and the seats springs
I find myself in tears: I didn't know I knew
the alternating pull, jolt of the hooves.
The harvest done, on the last empty cart
we were allowed to bump on the loose grains
home with this rhythm, this pace, exactly this.

Harriet Proudfoot

Stranger
Across the room, there he is –
The Woodbine smoking between his fingers,
Khaki uniform prickly and baggy,
Distant, standing next to the brown settee
And the table laid for supper.
Last week he was metalled up
In a tank tracking the desert.
I'm his little girl,
His hugs smell acrid.

Return
Singing and high voices rise up the stairs,
Laughter from his womenfolk.
There's my uncle in our flat,
In his peaked cap and naval uniform
Back from the East –
Despised place of curried heat.
He's bearing exotic gifts,
White frilly finery, silver-threaded skirts,
All foreign to me.

Blitz
They said afterwards
That when Liverpool burned
Everyone turned out into the street
To see the glow in the sky.

Victory Day
Gaudy flags, waved by arms hanging out of windows,
Marching, cheering, bands loud and brassy,
Faces in distant grimaces.
Pressed in a crowd of big people,
I see up to their waistlines.

Post War
A Kodak Brownie catches us.
Children in clean rags,
Adults lean and shabby.
We're grinning in black and white,
Only hope colours our eyes.

    Joan Hoare

Suddenly today I saw it
above the door. Stood, head tilted
back to check if eight red and white
flags still vibrated in the glass
cabinet in the stone-floored house.
I thrummed with joy remembering
that chubby pig-tailed ten year old
shooting through the cold quiet house.

Wooden bells, black – bulbous bottomed –
ridged; two-core flex – worn-naked wire
in cobwebs of old black cotton.
I planned the most effective route
to ring the bells and win the race:
left of the dining-room fireplace –
the inglenook fire in the lounge –
dash upstairs and start in the loo.

Spare bedroom – then theirs – flex knotted
between headboard and disused hearth –
Nick's room – faulty connexion there –
then mine – hidden behind the door.
Front door then back – past the bell box
through the scull'ry – past my mother –
backdoor bell push – past my mother –
in a triumphant, breathless skid

to check, head tilted back in glee,
how many of the red and white
flags still trembled? My friend and I
took turns 'till she made friends elsewhere.
And last Tuesday nearly sixty,
decrepit wiring connected –
I buzzed to see that little girl
and the vibrating bell box flags.

Jacqueline Bentley

When I walked in the big house –
so much at my sole command,
so much for my inspection.

Everywhere walls within
walls, doors heavy with purpose,
all there for my protection.

Decades on all is rubble,
suburban scrub, fit place
only for reaction –

Nowhere to stay away from,
nowhere to fear, or blame
for my imperfection.

*

An immense cream lion
on the great block of its base
presided over the place.

I stroked its curved tail,
traced its coiled locks,
gazed into its cold eyes.

And there across the steps
stood its identical twin,
fraternally forbidding.

How could I change and grow?
How could I ever escape
those stern exemplars?

*

Face pressed to the glass –
so little before the eyes
so much behind the eyes –

To be held within
the confines of that room
afraid ever to leave...

Once that face was mine
until I picked up a stone
and hurled it through the pane.

Sometimes even now
the slivers surge in reverse
and I'm back inside again.

John Killick

A child's smile spreads wide
In the wild of the woods
Where she defends her friends
From unseen foes
With sticks and stones on loan
From imps, pixies and
Fairy cakes baked into butterflies
With fingers sliding inside the ceramic bowl
As the mixture always tastes sweeter
Raw, like the scuffed knees
From out of control roller skates
Responding to the ice cream van's siren call
Of strawberry syrup smothered 99s
Or Mr Whippys served into wafers shaped like
Shells strewn across the beach
As if precious gems littering the sand
From a ship wrecked across the rocks that
House mean and green crabs who
Come home in buckets that once
Helped build the bestest sandcastle in the world
Draped with seaweed, too slimy to stay on
Spades beat diamonds but not hearts
To win the mountain of two pence pieces
Piled on the tablecloth competing with
Part assembled Airfix models and
Sindy whose hair's been styled into fluffy
Hamsters brought home from school for a lost weekend
Of sunflower seeds and freedom
To explore uncharted rooms and curtains that
Cascade like velvet waterfalls onto stone floors as shiny as
Conkers clonking in the playground, hardened by
Vinegar intended for Friday's treat of chips and
Roly-polys leaving grass stains on bodies
Spinning as fast as cheap plastic windmills
On seaside promenades where arcade claws
Tenderly brush the heads of stuffed teddy bears
Conscripted to join their fellow soldiers
In the wild, wild woods.

Anne-Marie Jordan

A b C d e f
g h i j
k l m n o
P q u r s t
u v u X
y z

IX

Blossom, said the child for the first time in his life
standing solid on small feet
dividing pleasure between two distinct syllables,
making a sullen day sizzle.

Blossom, again, reflectively, relishing rhythm
the releasing of lips, the plosive,
the up-down waggle of a four-year tongue
closing behind teeth and tapping them.

Every time we see some you must say 'blossom'
he ordered, savouring the stop of air,
the hum and vibration, the drop of pitch
in the latest addition to the inventory.

Blossom, we said together while I
considered the heart-stopping precision
of his mouth curving round *vinegar*
sobriquet, oubliette and *colonisation.*

Lyn White

She sees them everywhere.
Her universe
is twelve months old,
is populated by
an invisible colony
of cats.

They grin from where
they hang, upside down
on the ceiling,
glide elegantly
past her cot,
tread lightly
on the virgin fabric
of her dreams.

They are her North,
her South, her East
and West;
at twelve months old,
the only word
she knows is cat.

Jeremy Page

He can make sculptures
And fabulous machines,
Invent games, tell jokes,
Give solemn, adult advice:
But he is slow to read.
When I take him on my knee
With his *Ladybird* book
He gazes into the air
Sighing and shaking his head
Like an old man
Who knows the mountains
Are impassable.

He toys with words
Letting them go cold
As gristly meat,
Until I relent
And let him wriggle free –
A fish returning
To its element,
Or a white-eyed colt
Shying from the bit
Who sees that if he takes it
In his mouth
He'll never run
Quite free again.

Vicki Feaver

My fingers are pushing the pencil
up to the top line.
This must be a letter 'h'.
The line loops and falls
to the bottom line, then rises
into a smooth hump,
finally falls to a stop.

It isn't part of a word.
It's only a soundless shape.
As I watch. it's repeated again
and again on my pre-lined page.
We're sitting at rickety desks
making lopsided patterns
in a big curtain-less room.

Such a different thing, this,
from my secret writing at home.
That is real. That does things.
Though no one can read my page,
when I post it in the hollow tree
I see how a puff-ball swells,
how flocks of birds tack and veer.

Anne Cluysenaar

Our grandson crafts his words with thoughtful
intensity; scribes through the plastic stencil,
then cuts round them, practising
precision with adult scissors.

They wait in pockets round the house:
on the stairs are *Ryan Air* and *Easy Jet*,
sausages and *fountain* on the kitchen windowsill.
Herostar is on the hall floor.
After breakfast we have *Bovril* and *Marmite*,
from the giant atlas, *Black* and *Caspian Sea*.

His teacher in France would not approve of
the aid of a stencil, rather he should labour
forming words himself. I want to teach him:
facetious, crepuscular, exigency
but there's time enough for these.

He garners his words in a small paper
carrier bag together with a plastic
ruler and souvenir postcard of a train.
Racing car is on the grid to add.

Driving out for the day
we are just turning a corner
when he cries out from
the back, Grandma, Grandma,
I've left my words behind.

I smile to myself
remembering the journey,

It's OK Niko, it's OK
don't worry they'll be safe there
they'll always be there,
you'll always have them.

Sue Sills

I move out onto the lake,
noises under the ice *ping, ping*
beneath my feet. Walking
at first, I break

into shaky strides,
glide away from shore

to carve figure 8s,
even my nickname, *Patty* –
(possible in cursive).

What fun it is to cross
the T's!

I use the frozen lake
as my blackboard,
scritch-scratching
the cold

as I know it now, at nine.
Behind me,

my trail of words, numbers,
whatever it is I need to scrawl.

Freestyle, I practise falling,
getting up –

slashing my way over ice
lit by the setting sun, light
of the fast-rising moon.

Patricia Zontelli

You've been playing on the sofa, hauling yourself up
to laugh at your reflection on the wall behind,
smacking it with small sharp hands.
You turn, radiant:

> *I go bangbang on the mirror.*

Stunned, I see stars shooting, comet-tails.
Words have sparkled in isolation – a skyful of them, to be sure:

> *Christmas*
> 　　　　　　*helicopter*
> 　　*aqueduct*

household objects, and the name of every animal under the sun.
Somehow you've related the crude flatness of your picture books
to the real world. And your memory is cosmic. But:

> *I go bangbang on the mirror.*

That's the first full sentence of yours I've heard.

Happily, we bash hell out of it together
before you turn again, distracted by the glooming window.
　Moon
you say, like Ted Hughes' little Frieda.
Sometimes we've seen it there, but now I must explain:
those several satellites tonight come from this very room,
bounced by magic beyond the darkness of the glass.

Because you're a genius, you understand.
　Mirror
you say, and we wave at ourselves
arriving and departing among the moons.

> *Joanna Field*

for Joseph

For your first Christmas, you were given
a basket made from wicker
its contents most mysterious:
> a dark wooden stick for tapping a tune
> a piece of crumpled greaseproof
> > that grumbled at your touch,
> a rag of purple stuff
> a book of blank pages to rifle
> a balloon egg whisk to rattle…

You bit and licked and twisted
to gauge their size, their smell, their feel,
mastering this knobbly mess –
> > were they real?

For your fourth birthday I give you
another set of discoveries gathered
here on one plain page, adventures in store
and moments you can't yet imagine:

> flying a bold blue kite and
> finding the gulls soar higher;
> defying gravity on your first bike
> castles in a coal fire;
> the universe trapped in a snowflake,
> why a ball will bounce, but a bat will whack,
> the opaque sun and silver moon
> hung in an open sky,
> one saying hello, one yawning goodbye;
> foaming waves fingering your chest;

> the possibility of mermaids.

Judith Dimond

Some might call it singing when
amongst the trees
Ruby starts into her impromptu for the day,
among flowers she hardly notices
nearby the company of adults,
grandly, unmelodically
announcing syntax.
Ruby who knows
something about interval,
heavy with hairgrips and amongst flowers,
which she doesn't notice not even roses,
not even Ruby-high delphinium, acers
started into syntax
impromptu Ruby
joins words.
And of course she has on her best dress
since if nobody said so
this is Rubyday, the day Ruby,
as the adults recognise,
assembles sound,
deviant of course
among the roses,
acers nobody notices,
Ruby, suddenly unmelodically,
impromptu syntax on show.
Among adults who know the moment,
the day Ruby joins the language,
extravagant, impromptu,
amongst words,
and some might call it singing among the trees,
albeit grandly, unmelodically,
but this is Ruby
and today is Rubyday
and this is Ruby's song.
Which she announces not noticing the adults,
far away now from the city,
gathered amongst the roses
about which nobody cares,
acers upstaged by Ruby,
caught on her dress and in her hairgrips
grandly suddenly happy
amongst all those words.
Ruby don't stop,
not always everyday will be Rubyday,
deviate though Ruby,
hitch that dress,
here now among the syntax,

impromptu, unmelodically.
In your own time
sweetheart
make that noise.

David Herd

THE KALEIDOSCOPE

Some days mist wiped out the world that lay
below our house, days grey as the grate heaped
with the fire's ash, thick as the lumpy nastiness
of porridge which syrup couldn't disguise.

Those days weighed on me like art at school:
drawing cylinders, cubes, closed books on sheets
of off-white paper and not being allowed to touch
the boxes of crayons whose colours burned bright.

There was the day I knelt on the nursery lino,
picked up the kaleidoscope, peered into
its dark tube and gasped at the lime-green leafing
circles of purple petals, at the feathery threading

of moon crescents to stars and dots of gold.
One shake and this vision vanished but another
arose and with every shake another. I could erase
and create magical worlds whenever I chose.

Myra Schneider

Patience Agbabi is currently writing a contemporary version of Chaucer's *Canterbury Tales*. **Graham Anderson** teaches part-time in the Faculty of Humanities at the University of Kent. **Ian Badcoe** has been a biochemist, games-programmer and now writes CAD software / poetry. **Liz Bahs** is working on her first collection, *Swarm*. She is a teacher and PhD student of poetry. **Ros Barber** (www.rosbarber.info) writes books for emotional adventurers. Has cat. **Phil Barrett** trained as an artist and is a prize-winning, anthologised poet. **Fred Bazler** has published poetry and short-story collections, *I Once Saw My Heart* and *To the Skies*. **Jacqueline Bentley** is a psychotherapist in private practice who can see the moon on the sea from her bedroom window. **Mara Bergman**: poems published widely, and more than a dozen books for children. **Clare Best** writes at the top of her house, by a window overlooking Lewes and the South Downs. **Margaret Beston**: published in *Equinox*, *The New Writer*, *French Literary Review*. **Karl Birjukov** is a member of Poets Anonymous, based in Croydon. **Felicity Brookesmith**: member of Write Women Poets, has poems online and in haiku journals. **Victoria-Anne Bulley** began writing poems in early childhood, her first being about spiders. **Maggie Butt** is a widely published poet. Her books are *Lipstick* (2007) and *Petite* (2010). **David Callin** lives on the Isle of Man. **Caroline Carver** is a National Poetry Prize winner and official poet at Trebah Gardens, UK. **Nancy Charley** writes poetry and plays and is beginning to combine the two through performance. **Peter Clack** is a graduate of the Creative Writing programme of the University of Kent. **Anne Cluysenaar**: *Timeslips* (Carcanet, 1997); *Batu-Angas* (Seren, 2008); *Water to Breathe* (Flarestack, 2009). **Geraldine Cousins**: lives in Kent; three children; freelance illustrator; 10-year writer. **Martyn Crucefix's** new collection, *Hurt*, is published by Enitharmon Press. **Paul Curd** is studying for an MA in Creative Writing at Canterbury Christ Church University. **Michael Curtis** has given readings in England, Ireland, France, Belgium, Finland, Latvia and Germany. **Helen Davis** lives with husband, cats and books in Australia. **Clare Dawes** is working on a family saga, but enjoys any chance to write poetry. **Patricia Debney** writes mostly prose poems. Her new collection is *Littoral Drift*. **Judith Dimond** is a member of common room poets and author of *Gazing on the Gospels* (SPCK). **Miranda Dobson**: a second-year English Literature student at Newcastle University, born in Cheshire. **Marilyn Donovan** is working on a pamphlet inspired by Mondrian's paintings. **Val Doyle** was a freelance journalist who started writing poetry in retirement. **Hilary Drapper** is a member of Write Women Poets and has been published in *Connections* and *Equinox*. **Margaret Eddershaw**: poet, performer, traveller, fan of Man.Utd & Federer, lives in Greece. **Brian Edwards** is co-founder of www.afterliterature.org. He currently lives in Japan. **June English** organises poetry events and competitions. Her collection *The Sunflower Equations* is published by Hearing Eye. **Vicki Feaver's** latest collection is *The Handless Maiden* (Jonathan Cape). **Jo Field** is a grandmother. She lives in Deal and writes, with modest success. **Janice Fixter's** latest collection, *A Kind of Slow Motion*, was published in 2007. **Jane Francis** is a member of Deal Writers. **Wendy French** won first prize for a poem about her father in the Hippocrates Poetry & Medicine prize 2010. **Dorothy Fryd**: writer, performance poet, workshop facilitator, 2009 Canterbury Poet of the Year. **Lesley Fuller** lives in Whitstable and is a member of Whitstable Women's Writers. **Nancy Gaffield's** poem is from her collection *Tokaido Road*, which will be published by CB Editions in 2011. **Katherine Gallagher**: *Carnival Edge: New & Selected*, Arc 2010, www.katherine-gallagher.com. **Amal Garnham** lives in Canterbury and likes writing poetry about the people she loves. **Vanessa Gebbie** is a Sussex-based writer, writing teacher and editor www.vanessagebbie.com. **Alan Gleave's** work has appeared in various magazines; some poems are online at Message in a Bottle. **Daphne Gloag's** recent collection is from Cinnamon. First prizes from Poetry on the Lake and *Scintilla*. **Nicky Gould** lives in Whitstable & can see the windfarm from her window when she writes. **Gabriel Griffin**: poet & organiser Poetry on the Lake events, Lake Orta www.poetryonthelake.org. **Patricia Griffin's** childhood memories of Malasyia influence much of her writing. **Duncan Hall** lives in Bolton. **Harry Harris** is 62 and a member of Deal Writers. **Maggie Harris** has written five collections of poetry, a memoir, a dance-drama and short stories. **David Herd** writes poetry and criticism. He runs the Centre for Modern Poetry at the University of Kent. **Joan Hoare** will soon finish her MA in Writing at Hallam University, Sheffield. **Katie Hogben** likes experimenting with sound, tension and subtle sporadic humour in her work. **Mark Holihan**, a former Californian, is a poet and artist now transplanted to Kent. **Roger James** is published in *Fine Scribes*, *Logos*, *Night Train* and *Canterbury Festival Poet of the Year* anthology. **Maureen Jivani's** first collection *Insensible Heart* was published by Mulfran Press in 2009. **Anne-Marie Jordan** enjoys blogging, binging on box sets and reading in the bath. **Jenifer Kahawatte**: MA in Creative Writing, UKC. Bridport Prize runner-up 2008. **Lorraine Kashdan-Lougher** runs Kent-based live-lit organisation The Word and is the editor of *Social-i* magazine. **Jenny Kendrick** teaches AS & A2 English in adult education and is writing a PhD on interwar pony stories. **Anne Kenny** began writing in Melbourne during 2003 and has been unable to stop. **Mimi Khalvati** has published six collections. *The Meanest Flower* was shortlisted for the TS Eliot Prize 2007. **John Killick** is co-author with Myra Schneider of *Writing Your Self* (Continuum). **Becky King** is 20 and a student of English Literature at Cambridge University. **Frances Knight** is a musician, composer and songwriter living in Canterbury. **Bob Le Vaillant** has adopted four children and a Cocker Spaniel. **Gill Learner's** first collection is *The Agister's Experiment* from Two Rivers Press. **silent lotus** is a spiritual advisor & poet, resides in europe & usa www.silentlotus.net. **Virginia Lowe** *Stories, Pictures & Reality* (Routledge) www.Createakidsbook.com.au. **Richard Lung** also contributed to (May 2010) *Star*line*, US SF poets' journal. **John Lyons** is an award-winning poet and painter. He has published five collections of poetry. **John Mackay** is doing a PhD on American elegy at Birkbeck College, London. **Simone Mansell Broome** lives in West Wales where she's published three books www.simonemb.com. **Jenny Mayor** lives in Edinburgh, a heady mix of light, literature, hills & sea. **Shari-Lyn McArthur** was born on Vancouver Island & later co-founded afterliterature.org. **Alison McNaught** is completing a BA Hons in Literature and has been writing on and off for ten years. **Janet Montefiore** (b. Cambridge 1948) is Professor of English Literature at the University of Kent. **Chris Moore**: writer of confessional poetry and prose. Skeptic. Artist. Romantic. **Esther Morgan's** two collections are published by Bloodaxe. She lives in Norfolk. **Abegail Morley**: *The New Writer*'s poetry editor, is shortlisted for this year's Forward Prize Best First Collection. **Matt Moseman** a Cryptid; the american poet. **Andrew Motion** was Poet Laureate from 1999–2009. His most recent collection is *Laurels and Donkeys* (2010). **Gillian Moyes** has had poems published in various magazines and anthologies. **Ruth Padel** is the author of *Darwin: A Life in Poems* and of the novel *Where the Serpent Lives*. **Jeremy Page** lives in Lewes. His latest collection is *In and Out of The Dark Wood* (HappenStance). **Geraldine Paine** is widely published; her first collection is *The Go-Away-Bird* (Lapwing 2008). **Rachel Playforth** lives in Sussex and is published by The Frogmore Press. **Kyrill Potapov** is an English teacher. He was born in Moscow. **Caroline Price's** most recent collection of poetry is *Wishbone* (Shoestring Press 2008). **Harriet Proudfoot**: born in Elizabeth Garrett Anderson Hospital, now sadly demolished, still lives in London, teaches creative writing. **Lynne Rees** is a poet, novelist and editor. She lives in Kent and France www.lynnerees.co.uk. **Mark Roper** has published five collections of poetry, including *Even So: New & Selected Poems*, Dedalus Press, 2008. **Sue Rose's** debut collection will be published by Cinnamon Press in 2011. **Lucy Rutter**: poet, teacher, reluctant swimmer, easy cyclist and keen list-maker. **Sarah Salway** writes poems, novels and stories, and is the RLF Fellow at the LSE. **Carole Satyamurti's** most recent collection is *Stitching the Dark* (Bloodaxe, 2005). **Natalie Savage** takes the spirit of haiku and writes... of moments. **Maggie Sawkins'** collection *The Zig Zag Woman* is published by Two Ravens Press. **Mary Scheurer**, originally from Manchester, lives in France. She writes poetry and short stories. **Myra Schneider's** tenth collection of poetry is *Circling The Core* (Enitharmon 2008). **Derek Score** was born in 1931 and began to write when he retired from teaching. One collection, *The Dark Sargasso Sea*. **Derek Sellen**: born in south London, spent childhood holidays in Whitstable. **Bernard Sharratt**: b. Liverpool 1944. Taught @ Univ Kent. Retired. Gladly. **Andrea Shieber** from Herne Bay took a Combined Studies course in Creative Writing at UKC in 2006. **Sue Sills**, a grandma, loves words. She has taught, used and played with them. *Globule* is in her top ten. **Dan Simpson** is a spoken-word poet and writer. **Charlotte Sleigh** teaches and writes at the University of Kent. **Catherine Smith's** latest collection, *Lip*, was shortlisted for the Forward Prize for Best Collection 2008. **Emma Smith**: from Kent. Being daring went to Kent Uni. Still wants to be a writer when she grows up. **Ted Smith-Orr**: organiser at Poets Anonymous. Editor: football / poetry books. Read BBC–ITV News24. **Lorraine Spiro**: creative artist & teacher. Widely published in Cyprus and the UK. **Anne Stewart's** first collection *The Janus Hour* was published by Oversteps Books in 2010. **Gary Studley** teaches, writes and works for the Canterbury Festival Laureate Squad. **Margaret Swan**

writes with THE BELLYFUL, friends who are poets & also like to eat.
George Szirtes is a poet, translator and teacher of creative writing
at UEA. Latest collection: *The Burning of the Books and Other Poems*. **Kris Thain**
lives in a seaside town that forgot to close down. He writes poems because
he can't sing. **Moyra Tourlamain** is Canterbury Poet of the Year 2010 and
a Creative Writing MA student at UKC, after a career in communications.
Vivienne Tregenza is a Cornish poet working towards a first collection.
Debbie Turner: 51, biology graduate. Moved from Kent to north Norfolk
coast in 2009 with husband and mad dog. **Megan Watkins** lives and
writes in London and has two children. **Lyn White** lives in Maidstone
and belongs to the Kent-based common room poets. **John Whitworth's**
ninth collection is *Being the Bad Guy* (Peterloo, 2007). **Susan Wicks'** sixth
collection *House of Tongues* is forthcoming in 2011. **Vicky Wilson**: author
London's Houses (Metro, 2010), editor, educator, sometimes finds time for poetry.
Rachel Woolf has won awards with poems published in both Scots and
English. **Maggie Yaxley Smith** writes when inspired by the images and
stories of people, poets and nature. **Patricia Zontelli**: author of two poetry
books and has had poems in many journals.

Patience Agbabi 'North(west)ern' was first published in *Here to Eternity: An Anthology of Poetry Selected by Andrew Motion* (Faber and Faber Ltd, 2001). **Ros Barber** 'New Boy' was first published in *Poetry Review, The School Year* (Macmillan, 2001). **Jacqueline Bentley** 'The Bell Box' was first published in the Deal Writers anthology *Another View from the Pier* (2008). **Mara Bergman** 'The Summer My Father Died' was first published in *Ambit*, volume 120. **Clare Best** 'Drive Time' was first published in *Poetry Folio 60* (Kent & Sussex Poetry Society, 2006). **Margaret Beston** 'The Cranes' was first published in *The New Writer*. **Maggie Butt** 'Star-lit' was first published in *Lipstick* (Greenwich Exchange, 2007). **Caroline Carver** 'uncle boatman' was first published in *Jigharzi an Me* (Semicolon, 2000). **Nancy Charley** 'Sex Education' was first published in *Apprentice*. **Anne Cluysenaar** 'My fingers are pushing the pencil' was first published in *Water to Breathe* (Flarestack, 2009). **Geraldine Cousins** 'Three Ply' was first published in *Night Train 3* (University of Kent, 2005). **Martyn Crucefix** 'Empty the bath' was first published in *A Madder Ghost* (Enitharmon Press, 1997). **Michael Curtis** 'Christmas Concert' was first published in *In The Affirmative* (Redbeck Press, 2008). **Helen Davis** 'Never mind tomorrow' received an honourable mention in a poetry competition conducted by the University of Reading, 2002. **Val Doyle** 'The Onion Man' was first published in *The French Literary Review*. **June English** 'Silent Spy' was previously published in *The Sunflower Equations* (Hearing Eye, 2008). **Vicki Feaver** 'Slow Reader' was first published in *Close Relatives* (Secker & Warburg, 1981). **Wendy French's** poem was first published in *We Have a Little Sister and She Hath no Breasts* (Tall-Lighthouse). **Dorothy Fryd** 'Dusky' won third prize and was first published in a competition anthology of poetry by the charity Educating Kenyan Orphans in June 2010. **Nancy Gaffield** 'Sayo Amid Mountains' was first published in *Tokaido Road*. **Katherine Gallagher** 'A Girl's Head' was first published in *Fish-rings on water* (Forest Books, 1989). **Daphne Gloag** 'The Children's Charity Concert' was first published in *Ambit*. **Nicky Gould** 'Spoils of War' was first published in *Canterbury Festival Poet of the Year* anthology (2010). **Patricia Griffin** 'My Mother Had a Singer Sewing Machine' was first published in *Night Train 3* (University of Kent, 2005). **Maggie Harris** 'Valentine Birthdays' was first published in *From Berbice to Broadstairs* (2006). **Roger James** 'Black Swan' was first published in *Canterbury Festival Poet of the Year* anthology (2009). **Anne Kenny** 'Greenhow Grove' was first published *Canterbury Festival Poet of the Year* anthology (2009). **John Killick** 'The Big House' was first published in *Scintilla* 10 (2006). **Virginia Lowe** 'Real People' was first published in *MotherLode* (Poetica Christi Press, 2003). **John Lyons** 'The Builder' was first published by Smith/Doorstop Books. **Simone Mansell Broome** 'Medicine Bears' was first published on the www.jbwb.co.uk website in August 2007. **Shari-Lyn McArthur** 'Repast' was first published at Afterliterature.org. **Alison McNaught** 'Elephant' was first published in Australia in 2009. **Gillian Moyes** 'Original Sin' was first published in *boho women peeling oranges* (boho press, 2003). **Ruth Padel** 'Slices of Toast' was previously published in *The London Review of Books* (March 2007). **Jeremy Page** 'Seeing Cats' was previously published in *Juju*, Number 2

(summer 1999). **Geraldine Paine** 'Watching the News' was first published in
Envoi 138 (2004).**Caroline Price** 'Video Games' was first published in *Acumen*
1993. **Harriet Proudfoot** 'Bone Vibrations, Harvest' was first published in
Staple Magazine (1999). **Lynne Rees** 'Like the Sea'/'Comme la mer' (translated
by Christine Pagnoulle) was first published in *Words Unbound/Mots Déchainés*
for the MakeItReal International Writers' Exchange (2005). **Sue Rose**
'The Labour Room' was first published in *My Mother Threw Knives* (Second
Light Publications, 2006). **Sarah Salway** 'First Time' was first published in
The Kent & Sussex Poetry Society Folio. **Carole Satyamurti** 'The Day I knew
I Wouldn't Live Forever' was previously published in *The Forward book of Poetry*
(2008). **Maggie Sawkins** 'Our House' was first published in *Brittle Star.*
Myra Schneider 'The Kaleidoscope' was first published in *The Long Poem
Magazine.* **Derek Score** 'Aromatic Fever' was first published in *The Dark
Sargasso Sea.* **Derek Sellen** 'On Whitstable Beach' was first published in
Connections. **Catherine Smith** 'Snakebite' was previously published in
Lip (Smith/Doorstop Books). **Ted Smith-Orr** 'Red Cross' was previously
published in *Once Below a Time.* **Anne Stewart** 'Breasts' was first published
in *The Interpreter's House* (2007). **Megan Watkins** 'Sharing a Shell' was
first published online at *Message in a Bottle Magazine.* **Lyn White** 'Robert's
Blossom' was first published in *South* 32 (2005). **Vicky Wilson** 'Migration'
was previously published in *Line Dancing* (Categorical Books, 2009)

Lightning Source UK Ltd.
Milton Keynes UK
25 October 2010

161871UK00001B/16/P